MOUNTAINS TO OCEAN

A Guide to the Santa Monica Mountains National Recreation Area

BY RANDOLPH JORGEN

SOUTHWEST PARKS AND MONUMENTS ASSOCIATION

Tucson, Arizona

ISBN 1-877856-52-5
Library of Congress
Number 94-67914

Editorial
Sandra Scott, Susan Tasaki

Design
Gary Hespenheide

Typography
Hespenheide Design

Lithography
Lorraine Press, Inc.

Photography
© Tom Gamache/1995 for
Wandering Around
Outdoors

Illustrations
Cyndie Wooley, Christine
Wioch, Marlena Day

Maps
The DLF Group

Printed on recycled paper

Cover:

Inset (top), Santa Monica Mountains

Inset (bottom), Pacific Ocean, Sycamore Beach

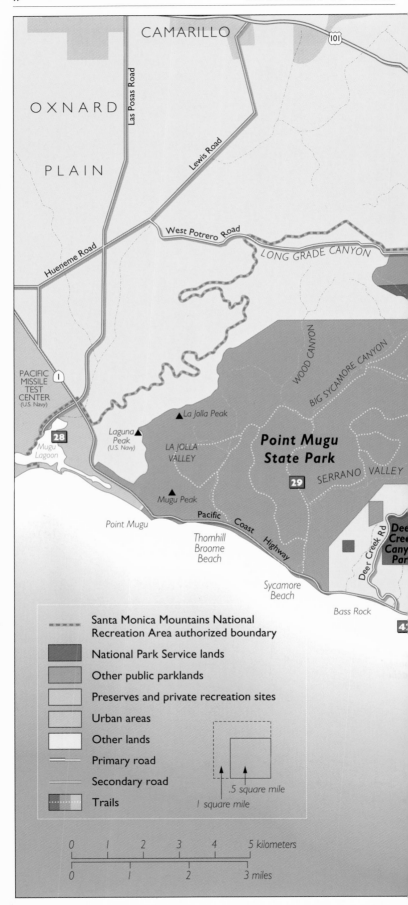

CAMARILLO

101

OXNARD

Las Posas Road

Lewis Road

PLAIN

West Potrero Road

LONG GRADE CANYON

Hueneme Road

WOOD CANYON

BIG SYCAMORE CANYON

PACIFIC
MISSILE
TEST
CENTER
(U.S. Navy)

1

▲ La Jolla Peak

Laguna
Peak
(U.S. Navy) ▲

LA JOLLA
VALLEY

**Point Mugu
State Park**

28

Mugu
Lagoon

29

SERRANO VALLEY

▲
Mugu Peak

Pacific Coast Highway

Point Mugu

Thornhill
Broome
Beach

Deer Creek Rd

Dee
Cree
Cany
Par

Sycamore
Beach

Bass Rock

4

- - - - Santa Monica Mountains National
Recreation Area authorized boundary

National Park Service lands

Other public parklands

Preserves and private recreation sites

Urban areas

Other lands

Primary road

Secondary road

Trails

.5 square mile

1 square mile

0   1   2   3   4   5 kilometers

0   1   2   3 miles

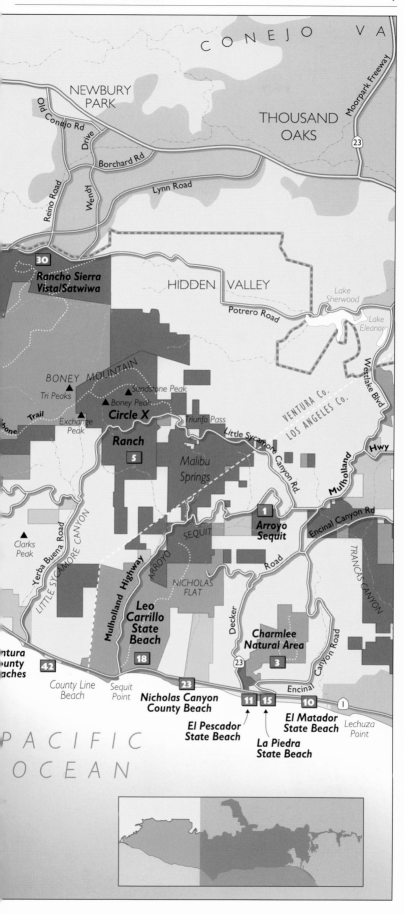

CONEJO VA

NEWBURY PARK

THOUSAND OAKS

Old Conejo Rd

Drive

Wendy

Borchard Rd

Reino Road

Lynn Road

Moorpark Freeway

23

30 Rancho Sierra Vista/Satwiwa

HIDDEN VALLEY

Lake Sherwood

Lake Eleanor

Potrero Road

Westlake Blvd

BONEY MOUNTAIN

Tri Peaks

Sandstone Peak

Boney Peak

Circle X

Exchange Peak

Trail

Triunfo Pass

Little Sycamore Canyon Rd

VENTURA Co.

LOS ANGELES Co.

Mulholland

Hwy

Ranch

5

Malibu Springs

Arroyo Sequit

1

Encinal Canyon Rd

Clarks Peak

Yerba Buena Road

LITTLE SYCAMORE CANYON

SEQUIT

ARROYO

Road

TRANCAS CANYON

NICHOLAS FLAT

Mulholland Highway

Leo Carrillo State Beach

Decker

Charmlee Natural Area

3

Canyon Road

ntura unty aches

42

18

County Line Beach

Sequit Point

23

Nicholas Canyon County Beach

23

11

15

Encina

10

1

El Pescador State Beach

La Piedra State Beach

El Matador State Beach

Lechuza Point

PACIFIC

OCEAN

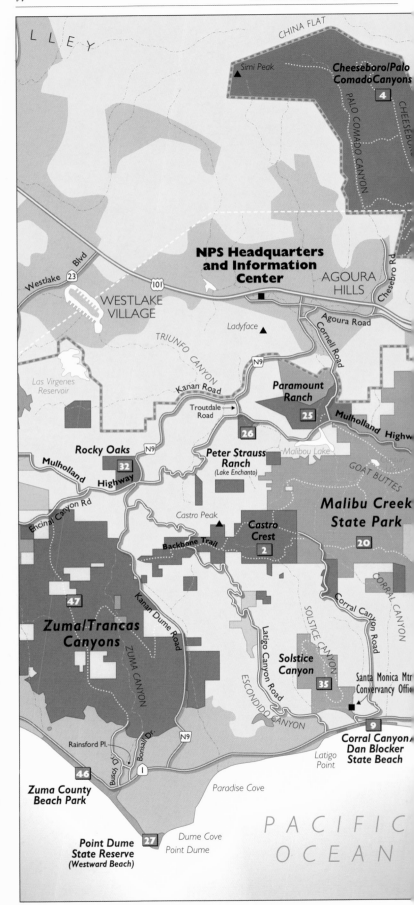

CHINA FLAT

Simi Peak ▲

Cheeseboro/Palo Comado Canyons 4

PALO COMADO CANYON

CHEESEBO

Chesebro Rd

NPS Headquarters and Information Center

AGOURA HILLS

Westlake Blvd 23

101

WESTLAKE VILLAGE

Agoura Road

Cornell Road

Ladyface ▲

TRIUNFO CANYON

N9

Paramount Ranch 25

Mulholland Highw

Las Virgenes Reservoir

Kanan Road

Troutdale Road

26

Malibu Lake

GOAT BUTTES

Rocky Oaks N9 32

Peter Strauss Ranch (Lake Enchanto)

Mulholland Highway

Malibu Creek State Park

Encinal Canyon Rd

Castro Peak ▲

Castro Crest 2

20

Backbone Trail

CORRAL CANYON

47

Kanan Dume Road

Corral Canyon Road

Zuma/Trancas Canyons

ZUMA CANYON

Latigo Canyon Road

SOLSTICE CANYON

Solstice Canyon 35

ESCONDIDO CANYON

Santa Monica Mtr Convervancy Offi ■

9

Rainsford Pl.

N9

Busch Dr.

Bonsal Dr.

1

Latigo Point

Corral Canyon / Dan Blocker State Beach

Zuma County Beach Park 46

Paradise Cove

Point Dume State Reserve (Westward Beach) 27

Dume Cove
Point Dume

PACIFIC OCEAN

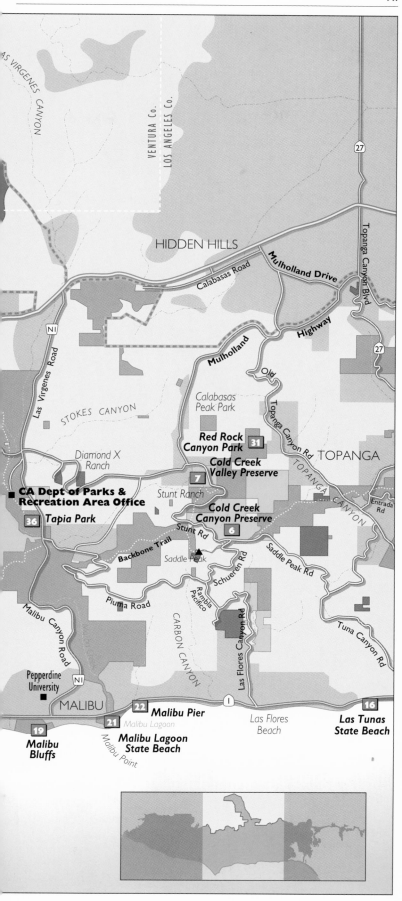

LAS VIRGENES CANYON

VENTURA Co.
LOS ANGELES Co.

HIDDEN HILLS

Calabasas Road

Mulholland Drive

27

Topanga Canyon Blvd

N1

Highway

Mulholland

Las Virgenes Road

Old

27

STOKES CANYON

Calabasas
Peak Park

Topanga Canyon Rd

TOPANGA

Diamond X
Ranch

Red Rock
Canyon Park

31

Cold Creek
Valley Preserve

7

TOPANGA CANYON

Entrada
Rd

Stunt Ranch

**CA Dept of Parks &
Recreation Area Office**

Cold Creek
Canyon Preserve

36 **Tapia Park**

Stunt Rd

6

Backbone Trail

Saddle Peak

Schueren Rd

Saddle Peak Rd

Piuma Road

Rambla
Pacifico

Tuna Canyon Rd

Malibu Canyon Road

CARBON CANYON

Las Flores Canyon Rd

Pepperdine
University

N1

MALIBU

22 **Malibu Pier**

I

Las Flores
Beach

16

**Las Tunas
State Beach**

21 *Malibu Lagoon*

19

**Malibu Lagoon
State Beach**

**Malibu
Bluffs**

Malibu Point

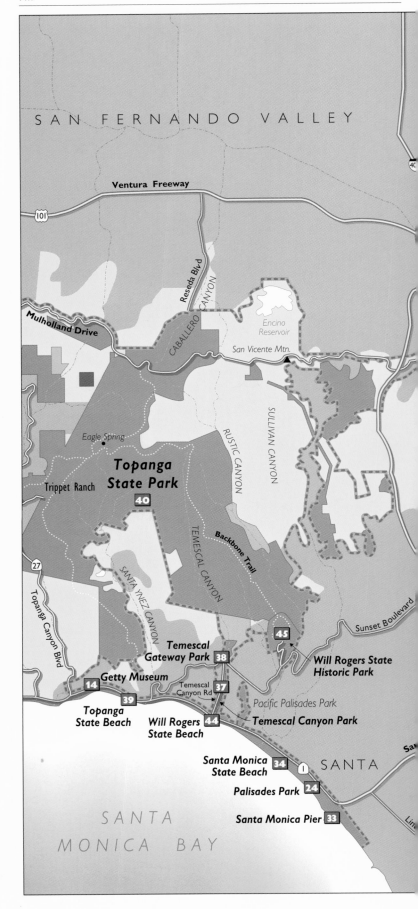

SAN FERNANDO VALLEY

Ventura Freeway

101

Reseda Blvd

CABALLERO CANYON

Encino Reservoir

San Vicente Mtn.

Mulholland Drive

Eagle Spring

SULLIVAN CANYON

RUSTIC CANYON

Topanga State Park

Trippet Ranch

40

Backbone Trail

TEMESCAL CANYON

27

SANTA YNEZ CANYON

Topanga Canyon Blvd

45

Sunset Boulevard

Temescal Gateway Park 38

Will Rogers State Historic Park

14 Getty Museum

Temescal Canyon Rd 37

39

Pacific Palisades Park

Topanga State Beach

Will Rogers State Beach 44

Temescal Canyon Park

Santa Monica State Beach 34

1

SANTA

Palisades Park 24

SANTA

Santa Monica Pier 33

MONICA BAY

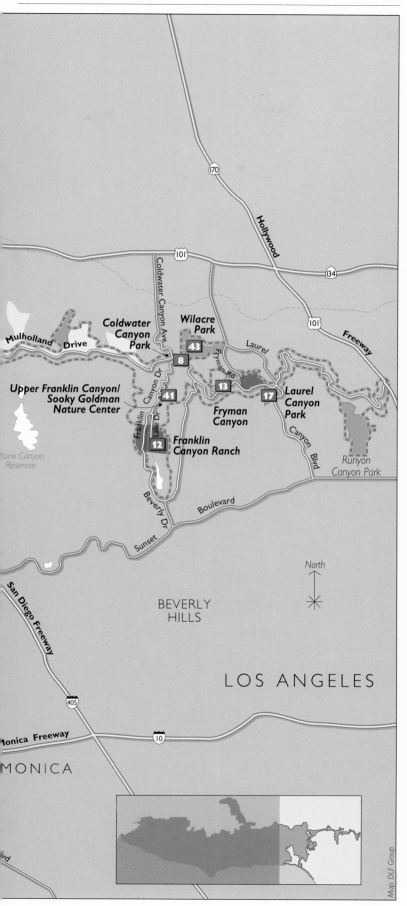

170

Hollywood

101

134

Coldwater Canyon Ave

Mulholland   Drive

Coldwater
Canyon
Park

Wilacre
Park

101   Freeway

43

Laurel

8

Upper Franklin Canyon/
Sooky Goldman
Nature Center

Fryman Rd

Canyon Dr

41

13

17

Laurel
Canyon
Park

Franklin

one Canyon
Reservoir

Lake Dr

Fryman
Canyon

Canyon Blvd

12

Franklin
Canyon Ranch

Runyon
Canyon Park

Beverly Dr

Boulevard

North

Sunset

BEVERLY
HILLS

San Diego Freeway

LOS ANGELES

405

Monica Freeway

10

MONICA

d

Map: DLF Group

	LOCATIONS	PAGE	TIPS AND NOTES
BEACHES	El Matador State Beach	39	Before swimming, surfing, or other water activities, observe wave and current patterns. Try your hand at sand sculpture. No special skills required!
	El Pescador State Beach	39	
	La Piedra State Beach	42	
	Las Tunas State Beach	43	
	Leo Carrillo State Beach	44	
	Nicholas Canyon County Beach	55	
	Point Dume State Beach	60	
	Point Mugu State Park	62	
	Santa Monica State Beach	72	
	Topanga State Beach	77	
	Ventura County Beaches/ County Line Beach	79	
	Will Rogers State Beach	80	
	Zuma Beach County Park/ Westward Beach	82	
BIKING	Cheeseboro Canyon/ Palo Comado Canyon	31	Santa Monica and Will Rogers state beaches have trails suitable for road bikes; all others are for mountain biking.
	Franklin Canyon Ranch	40	
	Malibu Creek State Park	47	
	Point Mugu State Park	62	
	Santa Monica State Beach	72	
	Solstice Canyon Park	73	
	Topanga State Park	77	
	Will Rogers State Beach	80	
	Zuma Canyon/Trancas Canyon	83	
BIRDWATCHING	Arroyo Sequit	29	In addition to the large transitory populations, a number of rare or endangered species nest within the National Recreation Area. Some parks offer free "Birdwatching for Beginners" walks. Check *Outdoors,* the quarterly calendar of events available at NPS Visitor Information Centers, for details.
	Cheeseboro Canyon/ Palo Comado Canyon	31	
	Circle X Ranch	33	
	El Matador State Beach	39	
	Leo Carrillo State Beach	44	
	Malibu Lagoon State Beach	53	
	Point Dume State Beach	60	
	Point Mugu Naval Air Weapons Station/Mugu Lagoon	61	
	Point Mugu State Park	62	
	Rocky Oaks	70	
	Solstice Canyon Park	73	
	Tapia Park	75	
	Ventura County Beaches/ County Line Beach	79	
	Zuma Canyon/Trancas Canyon	83	
CAMPING	Circle X Ranch	33	Only a few camps encourage RV use. See the index for specifics.
	Leo Carrillo State Beach	44	
	Malibu Creek State Park	47	
	Point Mugu State Park	62	
	Topanga State Park	77	
FILMMAKING SITES	Leo Carrillo State Beach	44	Check out the site used in the filming of M★A★S★H at Malibu Creek State Park.
	Malibu Creek State Park	47	
	Paramount Ranch	57	
	Santa Monica Municipal Pier	71	
	Upper Franklin Canyon/ Sooky Goldman Nature Center	79	
	Will Rogers State Beach	80	
	Zuma Beach County Park/ Westward Beach	82	

	LOCATIONS	PAGE	TIPS AND NOTES
FISHING	Corral Canyon/Dan Blocker State Beach	38	Please observe California Fish & Game regulations regarding catch size and limits.
	El Matador State Beach	39	
	Las Tunas State Beach	43	
	Leo Carrillo State Beach	44	
	Malibu Creek State Park	47	You can board a commercial sport-fishing boat at Malibu Pier for half-day fishing adventures.
	Malibu Lagoon State Beach	53	
	Malibu Pier	54	
	Point Dume State Beach	60	
	Point Mugu State Park	62	
	Santa Monica Municipal Pier	71	
	Ventura County Beaches/ County Line Beach	79	
	Will Rogers State Beach	80	
	Zuma Beach County Park/ Westward Beach	82	
HIKING	Castro Crest	30	Select footwear appropriate for the terrain. Know the first-aid basics. Don't take shortcuts or cuts across switchbacks.
	Charmlee Natural Area	30	
	Cheeseboro Canyon/Palo Comado Canyon	31	
	Circle X Ranch	33	
	Cold Creek Canyon Preserve	36	Investigate the Nature Center at Charmlee.
	Coldwater Canyon Park	38	
	Corral/Dan Blocker State Beach	38	
	Franklin Canyon Ranch	40	Topical hikes are offered in various parks. Check *Outdoors* for specifics.
	Fryman Canyon	41	
	Leo Carrillo State Beach	44	
	Malibu Creek State Park	47	
	Point Mugu State Park	62	
	Rancho Sierra Vista/Satwiwa	68	Trails for those with special needs are available at Upper Franklin Canyon and Malibu Creek State Park.
	Solstice Canyon Park	73	
	Temescal Canyon Park	76	
	Topanga State Park	77	
	Upper Franklin Canyon/ Sooky Goldman Nature Center	79	
	Wilacre Park	80	
	Zuma Canyon/Trancas Canyon	83	
HORSE TRAILS	Cheeseboro Canyon/ Palo Comado Canyon	31	If your horse kicks, warn others by tying a red flag to its tail.
	Franklin Canyon Ranch	40	
	Malibu Creek State Park	47	
	Point Mugu State Park	62	
	Topanga State Park	77	
	Will Rogers State Beach	80	
	Zuma Canyon/Trancas Canyon	83	
SCUBA DIVING	El Matador State Beach	39	Rocky reefs and kelp forests are home to an interesting variety of sea life.
	La Piedra State Beach	42	
	Las Tunas State Beach	43	
	Leo Carrillo State Beach	44	
	Nicholas Canyon County Beach	55	
	Point Dume State Beach	60	
	Zuma Beach County Park/ Westward Beach	82	
SURFING	Leo Carrillo State Beach	44	Currents and waves can be treacherous; match the area to your level of experience.
	Malibu Lagoon State Beach	53	
	Nicholas Canyon County Beach	55	
	Santa Monica State Beach	72	
	Topanga State Beach	77	
	Ventura County Beaches/ County Line Beach	79	

	LOCATIONS	PAGE	TIPS AND NOTES
SWIMMING	Corral Canyon/Dan Blocker State Beach	38	Be sure to swim within sight of a lifeguard. Cold water and rip currents can be hazardous.
	El Matador State Beach	39	
	Leo Carrillo State Beach	44	
	Zuma Beach County Park/ Westward Beach	82	
TIDEPOOLING	El Matador State Beach	39	The delicate fronds of sea anemone and the bright orange of starfish enliven tidepools. Take time to observe them.
	El Pescador State Beach	39	
	La Piedra State Beach	42	
	Leo Carrillo State Beach	44	
	Point Dume State Beach	60	
	Topanga State Beach	77	
WHALE WATCHING	Charmlee Natural Area	30	Migration patterns bring whales nearest the coast December through February. Use binoculars for better sighting.
	Leo Carrillo State Beach	44	
	Point Dume State Beach	60	
	Point Mugu State Park	62	
WILDFLOWERS	Castro Crest	30	The most brilliant spring wildflower displays follow wet winters. Collect flowers with your camera rather than your hands.
	Charmlee Natural Area	30	
	Circle X Ranch	33	
	Leo Carrillo State Beach	44	
	Malibu Creek State Park	47	
	Point Dume State Beach	60	
	Solstice Canyon Park	73	
WILDLIFE	Cheeseboro Canyon/ Palo Comado Canyon	31	When you go into protected areas, you are entering the animals' world. Enjoy your visit, but be aware of your surroundings.
	Leo Carrillo State Beach	44	
	Malibu Creek State Park	47	
	Point Dume State Beach	60	
	Point Mugu Naval Air Weapons Station/Mugu Lagoon	61	
	Point Mugu State Park	62	Take a notebook and record your impressions or make a few sketches.
	Solstice Canyon Park	73	
	Topanga State Park	77	
	Zuma Beach County Park/ Westward Beach	82	
	Zuma Canyon/Trancas Canyon	83	
AND MORE . . .	• **Amusement Park** Santa Monica Municipal Pier	71	At Laurel Canyon, "Dog Park," dogs are allowed off-leash during certain hours; check entry for specifics.
	• **Art** J. Paul Getty Museum	41	
	• **Family Attractions** Palisades Park	56	Palisades Park has a recreation center for seniors and an intriguing "Camera Obscura."
	• **Native American Indian Cultural Activities** Rancho Sierra Vista/Satwiwa	68	Picnicking is allowed in most areas; check park entry for specific details.
	• **Fun for Dogs** Laurel Canyon Park	43	
	• **Windsurfing** Leo Carrillo State Beach	44	Rocky Oaks is considered to be one of the most pleasant picnic sites.

Part I

An Introduction

Between their high, rugged, and wild western end near Point Mugu in Ventura County and their urban eastern end in the Hollywood Hills, southern California's Santa Monica Mountains encompass a range of astonishingly diverse and beautiful natural environments. Now the setting of some of the world's most dynamic cultures, the mountains also bear evidence of a rich cultural past.

For more than ten thousand years, long before modern visitors, the mountains were home to two advanced Native American Indian tribes, the Chumash and the Tongva/Gabrieliño people. Later, the Spanish established large ranchos in the mountains, followed by a few hardy Americans who made their livings ranching and farming in remote valleys.

Around the turn of the twentieth century, the mountains' beauty, variety, and wild isolation attracted new residents. Filmmakers found the mountains' varied terrain and mild climate ideal for the creation of cinematic illusions. Artists and writers built residential retreats here, as did religious groups. An estimated eighty thousand people now live within the park boundary.

Photo previous page: California sycamores and ground fog, Peter Strauss Ranch

The Lay of the Land

The Santa Monica Mountains stretch for forty-six miles, from Griffith Park in the Hollywood Hills to Point Mugu at the Pacific Ocean. In the east, they form a slender wedge a few hundred feet high that almost pierces the heart of downtown Los Angeles. They rise like an island, separating Los Angeles from the alluvial plain of the suburban San Fernando Valley. This is the mountain back-drop of brushland and wooded canyon from which California has derived Hollywood, Beverly Hills, Benedict Canyon, Beverly Glen, Laurel Canyon, and other posh, world-renowned neighbor-hoods. The Mulholland Scenic Highway was created in 1923 to encourage Los Angeles residents to discover the mountains.

Slightly farther west, the mountains reach their full width of approximately eight miles, much of which is spanned by the vast Topanga State Park, a virtual wilderness of chaparral and stony prominences almost entirely within the city limits of Los Angeles.

The middle section of the mountain range is a maze of canyons rolling south to the sea, gentle hills of live oak woodlands, and high peaks of the Castro Crest and Saddle Peak areas. Here is the Malibu Creek watershed, largest in the region and the only one to cut completely through the mountains; it is home to the southernmost spawning run of steelhead trout in the U.S. Seven-thousand-acre Malibu Creek State Park dominates parklands here, and offers some astonishingly beautiful and isolated terrain within a relatively small area. Even wilder are the large but little-known parklands of Zuma and Trancas canyons, administered by the National Park Service.

The western end of the Santa Monicas is the most remote from big-city influences and among the least developed. Here, the moun-tains reach 3,111 feet, their high-est point, at Sandstone Peak in Circle X Ranch, a National Park Service property. Adjacent fifteen-thousand-acre Point Mugu State Park has the mountains' only des-ignated wilderness, and offers

San Fernando Valley from Saddle Peak, Santa Monica Mountains

seventy-five miles of trails and fire roads through sycamore-lined streams, native grasslands, and secluded gorges.

On their southern edge, the mountains edge out the plains of the L.A. metropolitan area and meet the Pacific at Santa Monica and Pacific Palisades, forming the famous Malibu coast. In contrast to most of the southern California coast, the forty-six-mile Malibu coast runs east to west, first along the broad, sheltered reach of Santa Monica Bay to Point Dume, then along the rougher, more open ocean west to Point Mugu. The name "Malibu" is practically syn- onymous with movie stars, surf- ing, dazzling white beaches, and mountain estates overlooking the sea.

Along their northwest flank, the Santa Monicas border a series of inland valleys that once were the stronghold of the great valley oak savannas, but which are now the cities of Newbury Park, Thousand Oaks, Westlake Village, and Agoura Hills. Only through the narrow sliver of land at the National Park Service- administered Cheeseboro and Palo Comado canyons, by way of the Simi Hills and Santa Susana Mountains, do the Santa Monicas

The National Recreation Area

In November 1978 Congress established the Santa Monica Mountains National Recreation Area to protect the mountains' natural, cultural, and aesthetic resources and to preserve open space for recreation and for public-health value, an airshed for the southern California met- ropolitan area.

Although overseen by the National Park Service, the juris- dictions of the more than sixty other governmental agencies at work here remain unchanged. Congress recognized that peo- ple, private property, govern- ment operations, and commerce are inherent parts of the area. The National Park Service seeks to promote its goals by coordi- nating planning and activi- ties with other agencies, acquiring new parklands where necessary to relieve land-use

Boney Mountain, Rancho Sierra Vista/Satwiwa

conflicts, and educating the public about the mountains.

About one hundred fifty thousand acres fall within the boundary, which includes all of the Santa Monica Mountains from the Hollywood Freeway west as well as all of the Malibu connect with the inland mountain province.

Finally, on the west lies the Oxnard Plain, where suburban tract home developments now rapidly march toward the mountains' boundary. In the process, they are taking over some of the world's richest agricultural soils.

People and the Mountains

The twelve million people in the surrounding Los Angeles metropolitan area are fortunate to have on their doorstep more than sixty thousand acres of the Santa Monica Mountains and their beaches, now protected as public parks. The area's recreational opportunities help define the casual outdoor lifestyle that is southern California.

Each year, more than thirty million people visit the beaches. Many more hike, bike, or ride hundreds of miles of mountain trails, or drive the twisting, narrow, and scenic mountain roads. Camping, birdwatching, and wildflower-gazing are popular. Sites for picnics, weddings, and group activities abound, and the mountains have long been preferred venues for cultural events, such as fairs and concerts. Park coast. More than sixty thousand of these acres are now held as public parklands, with about fifteen thousand more expected to be acquired.

The greatest number of parklands are administered by the California Department of Parks and Recreation, followed by the National Park Service, the Santa Monica Mountains Conservancy, Los Angeles County Parks and Recreation Department, Los Angeles City Department of Recreation and Parks, Los Angeles County Beaches and Harbors, and several agencies with lesser holdings.

Note that regulations may differ from park to park, depending on the administering agency; be sure to determine regulations in the areas you visit.

National Park Service ranger and school group, Rancho Sierra Vista/Satwiwa

rangers and volunteer naturalists offer free educational programs to the general public, as well as special programs for children and the handicapped.

Climate

The Santa Monica Mountains have what is known as a Mediterranean climate—hot, almost rainless summers and cool, wet winters—in common with a few other semiarid, subtropical areas in the world, including the Mediterranean Sea, central Chile, southern and southwestern Australia, and South Africa. The land mass of these regions totals only about 3 percent of the world's land area, and is found in the middle latitudes, at around thirty-three degrees.

A major climate-shaping influence here is the Pacific High, a semipermanent high pressure cell of stable, warm, dry air that hovers over the ocean nearby. It is responsible for the absence of

Air Pollution

In the Los Angeles metropolitan region, some eight million cars are driven an estimated 213 million miles each day. The staggering amount of combustion generated by this activity, combined with emissions from trucks, buses, trains, planes, and motorized equipment, add an estimated 1,250 tons of noxious gasses and particulates to the air surrounding the Santa Monica Mountains every day. Stationary sources such as factories add still more.

As a result, Los Angeles has some of the worst air quality in the nation. Air quality standards for major pollutants, including ozone, carbon dioxide, particulates, and nitrogen oxides, are regularly exceeded. Acidic levels of rain, fog, and "dry deposition" particulates are at times as high as those found anywhere in the world, and can have the effect of vinegar on painted surfaces.

Air pollution damages natural systems as well. Chaparral plants develop yellowed, mottled, and twisted foliage and stems. Acid rain leaches nutrients from the soil, damaging plants, upsetting community dynamics, and harming amphibians.

Pollution is trapped over the L.A. and Santa Monica Mountains area by the same temperature inversion that traps the marine layer and causes summer fog and low clouds. Sunlight reacts with chemicals in the air, creating ozone and the brown smog that destroys the view of the mountains from L.A. for most of the year. Even on "clear" days, just as much pollution is being produced; it is simply diverted elsewhere by the winds. During Santa Ana conditions, pollution is pushed out to sea but eventually returns, and prevailing westerly winds push pollution through mountain passes and as far as the Grand Canyon, five hundred miles eastward.

Dense natural vegetation cleanses particulates and possibly toxic gasses from the air. It also contributes oxygen to the combustion-parched southland atmosphere.

Air quality has improved significantly over the last twenty-plus years. Stronger legislation has resulted in reduced auto and industrial emissions, and the switch to unleaded gas has also made a positive difference.

summer storms and the balmy, clear air that much of southern California enjoys during the late spring, summer, and early fall.

In late **spring**, approximately May through mid-June, fog and low clouds may last up to a week at a time, and temperature inversions can trap urban smog. Breezes grow strong by the afternoon, often sweeping the marine fog and clouds before them into the canyons. They then reverse at night, blowing down through inland valleys and canyons and out to sea. Temperatures range from sixty to eighty-five degrees Fahrenheit in the daytime and from forty-five to sixty-five degrees at night.

The Pacific High is strongest in **summer** and diverts storms away from southern California, resulting in a warm and rainless season. Inland, high temperatures are generally in the eighty-degree range, and only rarely over one hundred degrees. On the coast, temperatures average fifteen degrees lower than those of the inland valleys. Lows both on the coast and inland average in the mid-fifties.

Fall temperatures range from sixty-five to ninety degrees in the daytime; nighttime temperatures are between twenty to sixty degrees. Late fall brings summer-like conditions—bright, crisp days mixed with windy, rainy periods as winter moves in. Fall is generally considered to be the season of the infamous Santa Ana winds, although they have been known to occur in every month except August. These winds descend from hundreds of miles to the northeast, and are forced down mountain slopes and through the narrow passes of the San Gabriel and San Bernardino mountains. By the time they reach the coast, they may attain speeds of ninety miles per hour, and temperatures of one hundred-eight degrees.

Relative humidities as low as 2 percent complete the formula for extreme fire danger in a land parched by many rainless months.

Most **winter** days are calm, clear, and cool. Periodic storms bring virtually all of the area's rainfall during this time; an average of thirty-five days per year have measurable precipitation, with December and January usually the wettest months. Some winter storms are intense and produce the flooding and mudslides for which California is also infamous. Very rarely does snow fall. Winter lows are usually in the mid-forty-degree range, but sometimes drop below freezing, particularly at high elevations. Average highs are in the mid-sixty-degree range. As always, temperatures fall within a narrower range near the coast than inland.

Geology

The Santa Monica Mountains resemble a large, symmetrical arch, made up of layers of rocks of different origin and age, dipping downward toward the west. This arch can be clearly seen from the top of Topanga Canyon Boulevard looking north toward the San Fernando Valley. Although the Santa Monicas are a relatively young range that continues to rise from the sea and face the onslaught of erosion, their many faults, folds, downwarps, and varied strata reveal a complex geological history.

According to plate tectonic theory, the earth's crust is made of ten major blocks or plates that float on a layer of molten rock sixty to one hundred miles below. The movement of the plates as they collide, pull apart, or slide past each other generates earthquakes and volcanoes. The crust of the earth is crumpled and torn as deep basins are formed, and oceans recede while mountains rise.

The Santa Monicas owe their origins to the ongoing, gargantuan collision of the westward-moving North American Plate, which makes up most of this continent, and the Pacific Plate, which is creeping northwestward at a rate of about two inches per year. All of southern California west of the San Andreas Fault is on the Pacific Plate and, in several hundred million years, may find itself in the vicinity of present-day Anchorage, Alaska. The oldest rocks in the mountains began their journey near the Tropic of Cancer approximately 135 million years ago.

Oceans frequently covered the area of the Pacific Plate where the mountains now stand. Each time

The full range of geologic composition is present in these mountains. The tall peaks on the western end are volcanic. The central portion is largely sedimentary in composition. The eastern edge contains metamorphic and intrusive igneous rocks.

Erosion, the process by which the earth's surface is worn away by glaciers, wind, or water, is another powerful force. Once the rocks of the Pacific Plate are raised above the level of the ocean, erosion begins its work. Even as they emerge and pass through the surf zone, the mountains face a severe test from battering ocean waves. The Santa Monicas are rising faster than they are being eroded.

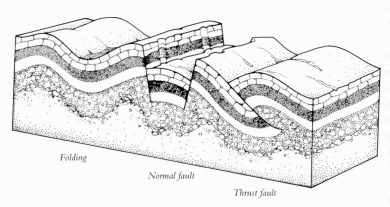

Folding

Normal fault

Thrust fault

an ocean came and went, new sediments were deposited, then turned into rock or eroded away.

There are three primary types of rocks in the Santa Monicas. **Sedimentary** rocks are created from sand, gravel, mud, or skeletons of aquatic organisms that collect at the bottom of a sea or lake or gather as a dune; minerals in solution (often calcium carbonate) cement the particles together. Many sedimentary rocks contain fossils. **Igneous** rocks are formed when molten rock cools beneath the earth's crust or emerges to harden above ground. When rocks of any type are changed by heat and pressure, they are known as **metamorphic**.

Water—falling with force from mountain heights; carrying abrasive sediment, rocks, and even boulders; and lubricating slopes— is the most powerful erosive force in the Santa Monicas. Soft rocks tend to be washed away, forming valleys or rounded hills, leaving harder rocks as cliffs and mountain peaks.

Many streams in the Santa Monica area have long, steep falls, with the erosive power to create a series of dramatic gorges. Malibu Creek (the only drainage to cut completely through the mountains) and Topanga Creek are thought to predate the latest mountains. They simply continued downcutting their existing channels as the mountains rose beneath them.

The mountains' southern slope receives more rain than their northern slope by capturing moisture from storms coming off the ocean. As a result, the mountains have lower, angled slopes and longer, deeper canyons on the south side than they do on the north.

Gravity takes a toll, large and small, on mountain slopes. **Soil creep** is a constant, imperceptibly slow, but important process in which soils slide downhill an inch or two a year without the aid of water. Landslides, an accelerated, dramatic version, send deeper layers of earth and rock downhill. Houses sliding down muddy hillsides are a familiar southern California phenomenon, and the still rising Santa Monicas are particularly prone to such movements. Occasionally, a large section of mountainside or coastal terrace will fall away in a slump, as happened in 1983, in this instance covering the Pacific Coast Highway at Temescal Canyon.

Debris flows form when torrential mountain rains encounter large surfaces of loose soil and rock. Then, an impressive volume of mud, sand, cobbles, and boulders moves down a streambed like a glacier in fast-forward. Such flows may be slower than flash floods, but are inexorable and have been known to swallow entire housing tracts, reminding us that the Santa Monicas are still a range in the making.

Life at the Seashore

Contrary to a widely held belief, the oceans are not boundlessly and uniformly productive. Rather, it is primarily the shallower waters near the edge of continents that support the life of the oceans. Here, sunlight penetrates to the seafloor and nutrients are brought in by rivers.

The coast provides precious estuaries, essential nurseries for ocean-going creatures. The shoreline is home to mammals, birds, and myriad other creatures and plants. The Malibu coast itself is a mix of rocky shore and sandy beaches bracketed offshore by reefs and kelp forests. Bluffs and small rock islands close to the shore are habitats for seabirds and marine mammals.

Waves and tides

Most ocean waves are generated by the friction of wind against water. In general, the longer the span of water over which the wind blows unobstructed, the larger the wave. Wind waves turn into lower, rounded swells that may travel thousands of miles with little loss of energy.

The Malibu coast is partly protected from northerly and westerly swells by the Channel Islands,

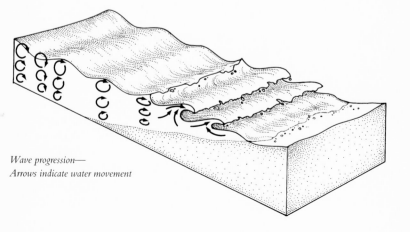

Wave progression—
Arrows indicate water movement

but may receive heavy storm waves from as far away as the Gulf of Alaska. In the summer, strong swells from southerly tropical storms make for good surfing.

Tides are cyclical changes in the level of the sea's surface caused by the gravitational pull of the sun, moon, or planets acting on the ocean masses. When these celestial bodies are on the near side of the earth, they tend to pull the oceans' water, raising the level of the tides. When on the opposite side of the earth, they influence tides toward a lower level.

The Pacific coast has what is called a mixed tide: two low and two high tides each day, all of unequal heights. Tides can be predicted with a fair degree of precision, but computations are site-specific. To predict Malibu tides, obtain a tide table for the nearest computed location, which may be Santa Monica or Los Angeles. Most such tables explain how to adjust for distance up and down the coast, and are available from local bait-and-tackle shops.

Kelp beds

In many areas along the Malibu coast, you will find beds of the large brown algae known as giant kelp, its "holdfasts" anchored in crevices in the rocky bottom of waters shallow enough for light to penetrate. Its long stalk, or *stipe*, reaches the surface, and large, wrinkled leaves are floated by gas bladders. Giant kelp stipes may be up to 120 feet long.

Kelp beds are the ocean's forests. The maze of stipes and leathery leaves waving in the surging swells provides food and a wealth of hiding places for ocean creatures. Kelp forests shelter nearby beaches by absorbing much of the energy of incoming swells and waves. When sea urchin numbers increase—a predictable consequence of the current elimination of their main predator, the sea otter—they can completely destroy a kelp forest by eating holdfasts or lower stems. The beaches are then left exposed.

In places along the California coast, large mowing machines harvest the upper parts of the kelp plant for conversion into fertilizer, nutritional supplements, and algin, an important stabilizer in dairy products and medicines and an ingredient in many paints and adhesives. Unlike terrestrial forests, kelp forests are short lived and may regenerate within ten years.

Beaches

The beaches of the Malibu coast consist primarily of sand and cobbles brought to the sea by mountain streams. The sand is light-colored as a result of its composition, which is mostly quartz and feldspar.

Most beaches consist of two major parts. The *berm* is the flat, above-water portion we are most familiar with, the scene of sunbathing, beachcombing, and volleyball. Just offshore and underwater at all but the lowest tides is the *bar*—a ridge of sand parallel to the shore, separated from the berm by a trough. Waves constantly shift sand back and forth between the berm and the bar. When waves are large and close together, as they are in winter storms, the berm is eroded and the bar builds up. Thus, in the winter our "beaches" (berms) virtually disappear, and we are left with narrow strips of cobbles. When waves are smaller or farther apart, as they are in the long swells of summer, sand moves from the bar to rebuild the berm.

Intertidal zone

The intertidal zone is the area of the ocean shore that is periodically left high and dry by outgoing tides. When the tide is in, conditions of uniform moisture, temperature, salinity, and oxygenation prevail. Water brings fresh food in the form of live organisms or detritus and removes waste products. But the surf also brings predators, and the force of crashing waves can crush or loosen plants and animals. When the tide is out, organisms face dehydration, the sun's ultraviolet radiation, exceptionally high or low temperatures, and land predators. However, despite the rigors of life in the intertidal zone, it is one of the ocean's most productive, with the greatest variety of life forms.

Estuaries

Estuaries are the meeting grounds of rivers and the sea, and lagoons are estuarine bays sheltered behind a sand spit. Tidal flats—mud flats left dry by low tides—and salt marshes are associated with many estuaries.

Estuaries are among the most biologically productive areas on earth. They enrich the ocean waters with their masses of rotting vegetation and animals, and act as ocean nurseries by providing food and shelter for juvenile sea-going fish. Estuaries are under attack nationwide by dredging, land development, water diversion and pollution, and the protection of the few estuaries that remain is all the more critical for the health of the oceans.

Mugu Lagoon is among the larger and more important estuaries in southern California. Other estuaries on the Malibu coast include Malibu Lagoon and ephemeral estuaries at Little Sycamore Canyon, Arroyo Sequit, Solstice Canyon, Zuma and Trancas canyons, and Topanga Canyon.

Patterns of life in the estuary are governed by elevation. In the lowest zone is the **lagoon**, an area of open water at most tide levels. Lagoons are home to small fish and are visited by ocean-going fish as well as harbor seals, who frequently choose the protected back side of sand spits as haulout sites. Microscopic plankton, algae, and blue-green algae multiply in the shallow, warm lagoon waters, recycling nutrients from decaying marsh plants. In turn, they are eaten by shrimp, snails, clams, and worms, which nourish crabs, fish, and waterfowl.

Slightly higher than the lagoon are the **tidal flats**, mud flats scoured twice daily by the tide

Sunrise, Malibu Lagoon

and drained by a network of tiny stream channels. With long periods of drying and submersion and unstable mud low in oxygen, the tidal flats are less productive than higher marsh areas, but still harbor many organisms. Plant life in the tidal flats is usually limited to sea lettuce and other algae and the abundant seed bearing eel-grass, an important provider of habitat and food for intertidal organisms.

The tidal-flat mud is alive with clams, cockles, oysters, ghost shrimp, and mussels straining food from tidewaters; urchins, sand dollars, and worms ingesting the mud in search of edible detritus; mobile crabs and shrimp preying on other crustaceans; and bacteria and fungi decomposing organic remains.

Salt marshes are the most productive and highest estuarine zone, and have the greatest variety of plant life. Organisms here must

has special salt-secreting glands on its leaves. Pickleweed avoids dehydration (which would concentrate salt) by virtue of its low form and small leaves. Its succulent stems accumulate excess salt on their tips and eventually shrivel and drop.

Marine mammals

Like humans, marine mammals such as seals, porpoises, and whales bear live young, have hair (or structures evolved from hair), care for their young, and have mammary glands that produce milk. Marine mammals developed layers of blubber to store energy and insulate them from cold waters, can restrict blood flow to extremities or outer layers to maintain core temperatures, and

*California
sea lion*

can stay underwater for long periods. All are intelligent and are thought to have descended from land-living ancestors.

endure extreme variations in salinity and moisture. Flooded only by high tides, they may be exposed to the air for up to ten hours at a time, subjecting them to strong drying winds and shifting sands.

The upper zone of the salt marsh has the greatest salt accumulation, and since salt tends to draw water from living cells, this zone is virtually a chemical desert. Reeds, bulrushes, and cattails avoid the salt by growing where fresh water streams enter the marsh. Other plants have evolved adaptations to the salt. Salt grass

Gray or brown **harbor seals** cruise sheltered bays, harbors, and lagoons in search of fish. Their lack of external ears identifies them as true seals. Harbor seals haul out on the beaches of the sand spit at Mugu Lagoon, pulling themselves along on their bellies with their front flippers.

California sea lions gather in great colonies on the nearby Channel Islands, and can sometimes be seen hauled out on rocks along the Malibu coast. Larger than harbor seals, they have external ears, a loud bark, and are curious and playful.

Locally, the most famous and sought-after marine mammal is the **California gray whale**. Three times during the past one hundred fifty years, gray whales have been hunted almost to extinction, but their numbers now seem stable. Grays, which grow to a length of fifty feet, are

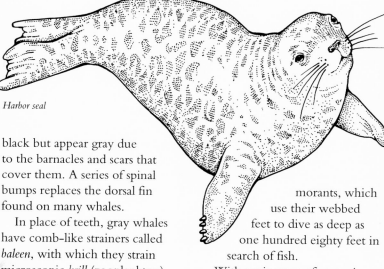

Harbor seal

black but appear gray due to the barnacles and scars that cover them. A series of spinal bumps replaces the dorsal fin found on many whales.

In place of teeth, gray whales have comb-like strainers called *baleen*, with which they strain microscopic *krill* (zooplankton) and algae. They propel themselves with powerful tail flukes. As they surface periodically to breathe, they expel warm, moist air from their lungs, visible as the familiar spout. Like other whales, grays are specially adapted to the cold temperatures of the ocean depths and navigate by use of *echolocation*, the bouncing of sound waves off objects.

Large family groups of gray whales, called *pods*, can be seen close in to shore as they travel from Alaskan waters to the warmer waters of Baja California for calving. Their departure from Alaska varies with food availability and water temperature, but generally, they can be seen on the Malibu coast from December through February; Point Dume is the best viewpoint. Their northern migration routes are farther offshore, and their movement is

spread over a six-week period starting in late March.

Seabirds

The Malibu coast is a popular winter stopover for birds traveling the Pacific flyway. Ducks, terns, loons, grebes, sandpipers, and plovers rest and feed on beaches and in the marshes. They join year-round residents such as killdeers, pelicans, and cormorants, which use their webbed feet to dive as deep as one hundred eighty feet in search of fish.

With a wingspan of up to six and one-half feet, **brown pelicans** are the largest fishing birds on the Malibu coast. By the 1970s, brown pelicans were in danger of extinction because agricultural pesticides had concentrated to dangerous levels in the food chain. After DDT and DDE were banned from domestic use in 1972, the pelican increased in numbers and is now fairly common.

Many shorebirds, such as **western sandpipers** and the **sanderlings**, stop here to feed on worms, crustacean larvae, clams, and crabs. Depth specialization—reflected in beaks of different sizes and shapes—prevents them from competing too closely with one another. These sensitive beaks allow them to pick prey from the surface of the beach or probe in the sand or tidal mud flats.

Birds of the marsh include **black-necked stilts** and

American avocets as well as **clapper rails** and **Virginia rails**. **Owls** and other birds of prey nest and hunt in the marsh.

Lagoons and tidal flats are frequented by birds that feed on plants and bottom-dwelling animals: the **common loon**, **surf scoters**, geese, and ducks such as **northern shovelers**, **mallards**, and **northern pintails**.

To many people, the seashore means **seagulls**. Most gulls on the Malibu coast are winter visitors who migrate north or inland in the spring to nest. Sleek and strong fliers, they kite effortlessly in the wind while searching for prey, and help to clean the beaches of debris.

Life in the Mountains

By virtue of their complex terrain, wide range of elevations and microclimates, and variations in soil types, the Santa Monica Mountains and their coast are exceptionally rich in varieties of plants, animals, and natural communities. That this ecosystem is still relatively intact and well-functioning is all the more remarkable considering the mountains' proximity to the nation's largest urban zone.

The natural world we know today is in many ways far different from what Juan Rodriguez Cabrillo, the first European known to visit the area, saw here in 1542. Then, the air was clean and wildlife abundant. In meadows, herds of pronghorn grazed amid lush perennial bunchgrasses mixed with a diversity of wildflower species and bulbs. There were probably fewer deer than there are now. Grasslands may have been maintained by frequent burning by Native American Indians, who used fire to encourage favorite plants and perhaps also for hunting. Plowing and overgrazing have since converted most grasslands to less-complex communities made up of a few annual exotic grasses.

Vigorous forests of imposing valley oaks grew in association with most grasslands. Most such forests have been lost to urban development, agriculture, cutting for charcoal production, and through depletion of seedlings by livestock grazing.

The San Fernando Valley, along with neighboring valleys, had a high water table that nourished extensive marshes. All such areas are now lost to channelization, pumping, and paving. It is likely that many mountain streams flowed year-round, and the *anadromous* (migrating from salt water to fresh water to spawn) steelhead and other native fish spawned in them.

Coastal waters were clean and fertile and were nourished by healthy estuaries at most stream outlets. Sea lions, otters, and whales were common, and massive schools of tuna and other large fish frequented the waters along the coast.

Current levels of bird life would be dwarfed by the clouds of waterfowl and other birds of earlier times. Bald eagles fished the coastal waters and inland marshes and streams. The mountains were home to the California condor, now gone from the Santa Monica Mountains. **Golden eagles** are now relatively uncommon, and several other birds, such as **peregrines**, **snowy plovers**, and **least terns**, are endangered.

Today, it is astonishing to realize that at the time of the arrival of Cabrillo in 1542, the mountains and plains around modern-day Los Angeles were home to what may have been the densest population of grizzly bears in the country. In the chaparral and grasslands, the bears feasted on abundant berries, tubers, and rodents. The last grizzly in California was killed more than seventy years ago. Even black bears are long gone from the Santa Monicas, although they still occur in the surrounding mountain ranges.

The larger parklands in the mountains preserve what is left of our natural heritage, but for wildlife in particular, patches

plants' and animals' adaptation methods. On land, plants typically provide the visible definition of a community; they are the food producers and the stationary elements. Animals, by contrast, tend to move about and may occupy more than one community.

Grizzly bear

of intact habitat must connect these parks with each other and with wild lands in the interior of California. Without such connections, animal and perhaps even plant species can become genetically isolated and gradually lose their ability to adapt to a changing environment. It is critical that remaining important habitats and corridors be preserved, for within a few decades, all human habitable open spaces are likely to be developed.

Natural Communities

Natural communities are populations of plants and animals in a particular area that are linked by interaction and mutual interdependence. The characteristics of a community are determined by the physical environment and by

Coastal strand

The coastal strand community occupies seaside dunes and sandy beaches. Plants here adopt a low-growing or creeping form to cope with the near-constant buffeting by strong winds and their shifting foothold in dune sands. The only significant remnants of the coastal strand in the recreation area are near Point Mugu and at the west end of Zuma Beach.

Key species in this community are the **sand verbena**, **silver beachweed**, **saltbush**, **beach evening primrose**, and the **beach morning glory**.

Coastal sage scrub

Coastal sage scrub is often called "soft chaparral," and is distinct from true chaparral. Coastal sage

(continued on page 18)

Fire

For thousands of years, fire has been an essential component of the natural process in the Santa Monica Mountains. Scientists believe that in prehistoric times, lightning-caused fires—beginning in the San Gabriel Mountains or San Fernando Valley and fanned by Santa Ana winds—reached the Santa Monicas in a wide front. At times, the Chumash and Tongva/Gabrieliño Native American Indians periodically burned areas to increase desirable game and plant species, especially in grasslands.

Fire-hazard periods begin in early May, when the annual grasslands dry up, and continue during the summer, when the land endures both higher temperatures and the long summer drought. Late summer is particularly dangerous, a time when high temperatures, drought, and the powerful Santa Ana winds coincide.

Chaparral is both highly susceptible and highly adapted to fire. Rich in volatile oils, it forms a dense cover with an abundant surface area of fine twigs and leaves. Scientists estimate that an average stand of chaparral burned about every twenty-five to fifty years before the arrival of European influences. This fits with the observation that stands of chaparral unburned for twenty-five to fifty years or more show substantial decrease in yearly plant growth and species variety.

Fire rejuvenates the chaparral, as well as elements of other local plant communities, by mineralizing organic matter into readily usable ash. Even in the absence of rain, within a few weeks after a fire chaparral species such as chamise, mountain mahogany, toyon, and laurel sumac sprout vigorously from woody stumps, or *burls*, buried in the soil; stump-sprouted chaparral species typically redouble their seeding efforts following a fire. Those chaparral species that have seeds rather than burls—California buckwheat, ceanothus, and big berry manzanita—need the fire's heat to break open their seed pods; germination follows the next heavy rain. The period fol-

New growth on charred sycamore, Point Mugu State Park

*Fire-scarred hillside,
Point Mugu
State Park*

lowing a fire is a wildflower bonanza.

The coastal sage scrub community, with plants of higher volatile-oil content, may burn more frequently than chaparral. Most coastal sage scrub species regenerate from sprouting of tubers and roots, as their seeds are easily killed by fire. But the year following a fire, regenerated shoots flower and seed profusely. Coast live oaks survive fire by sprouting from the stem or branches, even when all foliage has been burned off. But they may be killed if the fire is too intense, as happens when too much fuel has accumulated as a result of infrequent fires.

Fires in the valley oak savanna are fast moving and not very hot, and therefore are not threatening to valley oaks that grow there. Grasses are adapted to frequent fires. Annuals grow quickly from seed, and the above-ground parts of perennials, with their roots intact, sprout even in the absence of rain.

Most animals survive fires by fleeing or hiding in burrows. While after the fire population numbers may fall from lack of habitat and food in the short term, they later soar when the herbaceous cover grows, the heavy seed crop arrives, and insects return in force, all providing abundant food supply.

Fires also hollow nesting cavities in trees for birds and small mammals.

The advent of effective fire suppression techniques means that natural fires in the mountains were nearly eliminated and fires of human origin were quick to be suppressed. This caused the buildup of dangerous amounts of fuel. When such areas burn, the results may be catastrophic, uncontrollable fires that can result in personal property damage or loss of human life.

Too-frequent fires can convert chaparral, coastal sage scrub, oak woodland, and valley oak savanna to annual grassland.

The National Park Service, the Los Angeles city and county fire departments, and the Ventura County Fire Department are cooperating in the ongoing practice of "prescribed fires," fires that are carefully set during safe times of the year in areas with dangerous levels of fuel accumulation.

Fire is thus prescribed to prevent loss of human life and property and catastrophic natural fires, rejuvenate the chaparral and control alien species, improve wildlife habitat, and break the fire-flood cycle. Eventually, this cooperative program will result in a mosaic of different aged vegetation that will help keep wildfires to manageable size.

scrub plants range from one to seven feet tall, tolerate dry conditions, and grow best on dry, gravelly, and rocky south-facing slopes. Many are deciduous in drought or summer to reduce water loss. Shallow roots allow these plants to take advantage of light rains.

Key coastal sage scrub species include **California sagebrush**, **California buckwheat**, **purple sage**, **lemonadeberry**, and **laurel sumac**.

Chaparral

The word "chaparral" derives from *el chaparro*, Spanish for "place of the scrub oak." It refers to plant communities of dense, woody, mostly evergreen shrubs four to twelve feet high, generally with small, waxy, "hardened" leaves that resist water loss. Mature chaparral communities (at least ten years old) are thick and extremely difficult to penetrate. Chaparral plants are specially fire-adapted, and the community requires periodic burning to maintain health.

Chaparral stabilizes loose soils and improves rainwater percolation, generates oxygen, filters particulate air pollutants, harbors a wealth of small animals and birds, and yields a rich variety of wildflowers almost year-round.

Chaparral shrubs seem to prefer sites with little or no soil, where they send deep roots through cracks in the bedrock. There, they find water to help them through the long, dry summers; most plants are dormant in late summer and early fall.

Chaparral is the dominant vegetation type in the Santa Monica Mountains, as well as much of southern California. It occurs only in Mediterranean climates, and the national recreation area contains the largest extent of true Mediterranean chaparral preserved within the national park system.

In this community, key species are **chamise**, **black sage**, **big-pod ceanothus**, **greenbark ceanothus**, and **toyon**.

Grasslands

Grasslands occur on valley floors and low, rolling hills with heavy clay soils that drain slowly. Grasses grow quickly and their shallow roots take advantage of light rains. Alien grasses in the Santa Monica Mountains are dormant during the dry summer and grow from winter through early spring. Native perennial grasses are green at the base year-round. Grassland communities have been altered by heavy livestock grazing, plowing, burning, and the introduction of exotic species.

Grassland key species include **purple needlegrass**, **foothill needlegrass**, and **creeping rye grass**.

Oak woodlands

Oak woodlands are an important community for wildlife habitat, providing food, nesting and roosting sites, and shade. Their acorns were a crucial carbohydrate source for the Chumash and Tongva/Gabrieliño.

Interference with the normal fire frequency threatens oaks in some areas, and cities of the San Fernando Valley have been carved out at the oaks' expense. Oak seedlings are being destroyed by livestock grazing and by gophers, who increase unchecked due to elimination of their natural predators. At the same time, exotic annual grasses out-compete oak seedlings for moisture. The result is that we are missing generations of oaks, and are left with mostly two hundred- to three hundred-year-old trees that are losing vigor as their cores rot with age and fire scars.

The National Park Service and California Department of Parks and Recreation have undertaken oak-restoration projects at Malibu Creek State Park, Paramount Ranch, and Cheeseboro Canyon.

Key species here are **valley oak**, **coast live oak**, **hollyleaf cherry**, **poison oak**, **California bay**, and **coffeeberry**.

Riparian woodlands

Riparian woodlands are cool, moist oases in a sea of chaparral. They occur along the canyon bottoms, where surface or sub-surface streams are found nearly year-round, and may have the greatest diversity of plant and animal life of any community here. A canopy of broad-leafed trees

example of sycamore savanna; other good examples are at lower Zuma Canyon and Malibu Creek State Park.

Key species in the riparian community are the **sycamore**, **alder**, **black walnut**, **willow**, **mugwort**, **California bay**, and numerous **fern** species.

Freshwater aquatic

The freshwater aquatic community—commonly known as marsh vegetation—occurs in shallow pools, the edges of ponds, and in slow-moving streams. Like the lagoon, its salt-water counterpart, the freshwater

High Road, Malibu Creek State Park

shelters a layer of shrubs, such as coffeeberry, and a layer of herbaceous plants and abundant ferns. Plants in this community grow in proximity to the creekbed according to the degree of flood scouring they can withstand. Willows are among the more hardy.

Malibu Creek, Cold Creek Preserve, and Solstice Canyon have the best riparian woodlands. Big Sycamore Canyon in Point Mugu State Park has the finest

marsh supports a wide range of life, from bacteria, protozoa, and fungi; *planktonic* (floating) and filamentous algae; tiny crustaceans; unique aquatic plants; to a host of higher animals such as frogs, waterfowl, and the territorial red-winged blackbird. Pondweed leaves float on the surface of the water, connected to thick roots or tubers buried in bottom mud. Others, such as the tiny duck-weed fern and duckweed, one of the world's smallest flowering

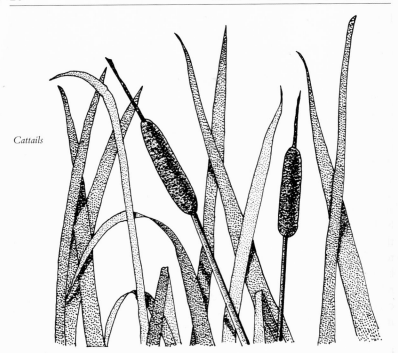

Cattails

plants, simply float about on the water's surface.

Many marshlands, especially those at the edges of natural and manmade lakes, are in transition from wet to dry land. Reed-like aquatic plants, cattails, sedges, and bulrushes for example, accelerate the process by stabilizing sediments and adding organic material. The pond (an artificial impoundment) at Nicholas Flat in Leo Carrillo State Beach, is the best example of this and of the freshwater aquatic community in the Santa Monica Mountains. The ponds at Rocky Oaks, Century Lake in Malibu Creek State Park, and La Jolla Valley in Point Mugu State Park are other examples of the community.

Key freshwater aquatic community species include the **bulrush**, **cattail**, and **sedge**.

Rock slope and outcrop

This highly specialized community occurs only on areas of otherwise bare rock, where the plants take advantage of crevices and rivulets of rain or other surface water to gain footholds and grow. Examples of the rock slope and outcrop community can be found in Triunfo Gorge near the Rock Pool at Malibu Creek State Park, at the Grotto in Circle X Ranch, and along the Mishe Mokwa Trail in Carlisle Canyon, also in Circle X Ranch.

Key species in this community are **chalk live-forever**, **club moss**, **lichens**, and **chaparral fern**.

Wildlife

Fifty-three species of mammals (including seven exotic species) live in the Santa Monica Mountains. This is an exceptionally large and diverse assemblage, given the mountains' proximity to a dense urban area, and attests to the rugged nature of the terrain and the diversity of plant communities. This mammalian bounty is another reason to preserve public parklands.

The **mountain lion** is rare, nocturnal, and shy; a few still live in the rockier and more remote parts of the mountains, especially around Malibu Creek State Park, Zuma Canyon, Castro Crest, Cheeseboro and Palo Comado canyons, Circle X, Topanga State

Park, and Boney Mountain. From nose to tail, it is typically seven feet long; the tail alone is three feet, almost one-half of the lion's length. It can weigh up to 125 pounds, and feeds on small mammals; it will also kill lesser predators such as coyotes. Deer are the preferred food, and when conditions are right, the lion can kill an average of one a week.

The **gray fox** is also rare, shy, and nocturnal, with a dog-like bark. It measures an average of three and one-half feet and weighs ten to eighteen pounds. Rodents, birds, reptiles and amphibians, and rabbits, as well as plants such as cactus fruits, berries, and roots, make up its diet.

The **coyote**, the "song dog," looks like a slender German shepherd and eats almost anything it can find, including plants, animals, and carrion. Coyotes prey primarily on rodents, but they may occasionally hunt in packs to kill larger animals.

The **bobcat** is cousin to the mountain lion and has a short tail and tufts of hair on the ends of its ears. Bobcats prefer rugged chaparral terrain and are abundant in

quently raids campsites right behind the campers' backs. Its splayed, flat-footed tracks are often found in the mud around ponds and streams, where it looks for its preferred food, frogs, fish, crayfish, and shellfish. It also dines on rodents, birds, and other small game. The raccoon is generally about thirty inches long and weighs an average of twenty-two pounds.

The **ringtail** is an uncommon cousin of the raccoon; almost half of its total length of thirty-one inches is in its tail, which measures about fifteen inches long. A small mammal, weighing in at a little over two pounds, the ringtail prefers canyon bottoms, and nests in hollow trees, rock crevices, and caves. A reclusive and strictly nocturnal hunter, the ringtail's diet consists of rodents, insects, and berries.

Badgers, squat and heavy-set with black-and-white-striped faces, are prodigious diggers. Because of the progressive loss of their grassland habitat, badgers are rare in the Santa Monica Mountains area. Although they are abroad in daylight hours, they

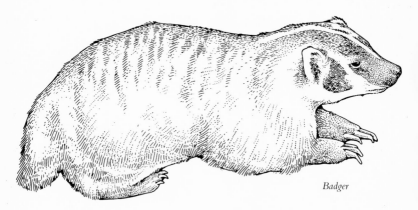

Badger

the Santa Monicas. The bobcat grows to three feet in length and weighs an average of thirty pounds. It takes game up to the size of small deer.

The **raccoon** is a bold and opportunistic carnivore that fre-

are primarily nocturnal and can sometimes be seen in Cheeseboro Canyon, Rancho Sierra Vista, Big Sycamore Canyon, or in grassy areas of Topanga State Park. Adult badgers measure about thirty-one inches long and weigh about twenty pounds, a weight they maintain on a diet of ground squirrels, snakes, mice, and rabbits.

The **striped skunk** is about the size of a very small dog, twenty-eight inches long and six to fifteen pounds. It is black with white stripes on the side of its back and tail and one white stripe down the center of its face. The skunk's unmistakable coloring alerts potential foes to the animal's special defense, and it also has a behavior that warns attackers off. When threatened, it will stamp its front feet then turn and raise its tail before spraying a noxious fluid, sometimes at a distance of several feet. A bath in vinegar or tomato juice is in order for the unfortunate dog or person who encounters the skunk's wrath. The striped skunk feeds on birds, eggs, rodents, and insects.

Mule deer are the mountains' largest *herbivores* (vegetarians). They seek cover in thick brush and in the understory of riparian woodlands, ever alert for mountain lions, coyotes, and bobcats. They are browsers, eating twigs, leaves, and fruits of shrubs and trees, and can weigh up to 200 pounds.

Desert cottontails are perhaps the most commonly seen herbivores. The smaller California vole, or **meadow mouse**, and **pocket mouse** are generally well concealed in the chaparral. One rodent you are unlikely to see but whose home you won't miss is the **dusky-footed woodrat**, or "pack rat." The woodrat chooses a spot under a tree or rock ledge and piles leaves, sticks, and other available material into a mound that may be up to six feet across and four feet high.

Long-tailed weasels are medium-sized predators with short legs, a narrow chocolate-brown body, and a long neck. They prefer rock or wood piles as habitats, and live on a diet of small birds and rodents, including mice, gophers, and ground squirrels.

Birds

About 384 species of birds (including vagrants) have been sighted in the national recreation area, and about 263 species of birds regularly occur here. In the annual Audubon Society Christmas bird counts, the Santa Monica Mountains and Malibu coast are consistently ranked within the top ten sites in the U.S. for variety.

Raptors, or birds of prey, are at the top of the food chain. They feed on rodents and small mammals, snakes, and other birds, and help to keep these populations in check. The Santa Monica Mountains have more species of nesting raptors than anywhere else in the United States (except the Snake River Birds of Prey National Conservation Area in Idaho) because of the wide variety of terrain and natural communities and the high productivity of those communities. The dense cover and numerous oak woodland hollows offer nest sites for Cooper's hawks, red-shouldered hawks, white-tailed kites, and owls. Rocky cliff faces provide golden eagles and prairie falcons with abundant sites for crevice nesting, and there are ample hunting grounds in grassland clearings.

The **golden eagle** is the largest bird in the mountains, with a wingspan of up to seven and one-half feet. Its greater size and flatter and more square wing profile in flight differentiate it from the large hawks (such as the red-tailed). With only an occasional flap of its powerful wings, it circles high in the sky searching for rabbits and large rodents, its chief prey. Although the golden eagle is rare here, your best chance of seeing one is in Cheeseboro and Palo Comado canyons or the Triunfo

Gorge area of Malibu Creek State Park.

The **red-tailed hawk** is often seen sitting on utility poles or in trees, or soaring in wide circles. This hawk has a rounded tail and a wingspan of up

Red-tailed hawk

to four and one-half feet. Because it occurs in many different color phases, it is often difficult to distinguish it from the red-shouldered hawk. Both species are important predators of mice, rabbits, reptiles, and rats.

Cooper's and **sharp-shinned hawks** are similar in appearance, though the Cooper's is larger, about the size of a crow. Both have blue-gray backs, rust-colored fronts with horizontal stripes, and small heads. Their short, rounded wings and long tails give them the speed and maneuverability they need to dart through the canopies of oak and riparian woodlands where they hunt small birds.

Still occasionally seen along high cliff faces, such as those of Boney Ridge and Sandstone Peak, are **prairie falcons**, cousin to the endangered peregrine falcon, which is often found at Mugu Lagoon. With long, pointed wings and long tails, both falcons are among the fastest birds in the world, attaining speeds in excess of two hundred miles per hour in *stoops*, or attack dives, on other birds, their preferred prey.

Small cousin to the prairie falcon is the **American kestrel**, or sparrow hawk. The kestrel has a banded *rufous* (reddish) tail and rufous wings. It is most commonly seen perched on wires, its tail occasionally jerking up and down, or *kiting* (hovering) in the air, searching for insects, snakes, and mice.

Great horned owls, barn owls, and **western screech owls**

Prairie falcon

hunt through woodlands and grasslands at night. Most owls have excellent night vision, but rely more on their acute hearing and asymmetrical ear arrangement to find prey in the dark. Owl feathers are typically "furry" on top, which silences the feathers as they slide over one another in flight and avoids alerting the rodents that are favorite owl prey.

The **turkey vulture** is head of nature's cleanup crew, feeding on *carrion* (dead animals). To distinguish its large, dark form from that of golden eagles, note that eagles hold their wings flat while soaring, while turkey vultures hold theirs in a V-shape and rock unsteadily from side to side.

The **common raven** is one of the world's most intelligent birds. At twenty-two inches to twenty-seven inches in length, this jet-black bird is larger than its cousin the crow, has a wedge-shaped tail, and a wider variety of calls. Ravens are often seen soaring with hawks and vultures, or tumbling playfully through the air. Ravens are *omnivores*, feeding on carrion, bird eggs, seeds, and small snakes and lizards.

The **acorn woodpecker** is the clown bird of the oak woodlands. You are certain to hear the scolding cries of these jaunty black-and-white "tuxedoed" birds with red caps as they go about their business of perforating oak and sycamore trunks to store acorns. Other woodpeckers of the chaparral and woodlands, including the common flicker, Nuttall's woodpecker, and downy woodpecker, bore for wood-burrowing insects rather than to store seeds, as does the acorn woodpecker.

The sounds of certain birds spell "chaparral" to experienced mountain visitors. The state bird—**California quail**—can be heard calling "chicago" from bush to bush. Quail travel in multifamily groups called *coveys*. The quail prefers to run rather than fly, and seeks dense shrub for cover.

Other characteristic calls from the chaparral come from the **wrentit**, with its accelerating series of short notes dropping in pitch, and the **California thrasher**. The latter is in the family *Mimidae* ("mimics"); a cousin to the mockingbird, it has its own wide repertoire of mimic songs. It thrashes through dead leaves and dirt for insects and seeds with its long, curved bill.

The tiny **Anna's hummingbird** gives a surprisingly loud, raspy call of "chee chee chee" as it scans its fiercely guarded territory of flowering shrubs. Hummingbirds co-evolved with tubular flowers—the flowering shrubs depend on hummingbirds for pollination, while hummingbirds depend on the flowers for nectar.

The **scrub jay**, a conspicuous—and sometimes obnoxious—resident of the chaparral and oak woodlands, is related to the raven. Its head, wings, and tail are blue, its underside white. The scrub jay makes a variety of raucous and grating calls as it glides over the brush or attempts to rob picnic lunches.

Amphibians and reptiles

Amphibians lead a dual life: most lay their eggs in water and the juveniles, such as tadpoles, live in water. Adult forms, frogs for example, come out of the water onto the land, but can also live in water, breathing through their skin. Adults are still generally restricted to moist canyon bottoms and ponds and can be found in stream pools, under rocks, or in moist forest or chaparral duff. Eleven species of amphibians, including the **Pacific treefrog** and the **California treefrog**, occur in the mountains. Despite their name, both most commonly live not in trees but on the ground or on rocks. With sticky toepads, they cling to rocks and shrubs, hunting insects. They spend most of their time out of the water, except from January to July, when they stay near ponds or streams for breeding.

The **California newt** is the only newt found in coastal southern California. Its naked, smooth skin (brown above, yellow or orange on the belly) easily distinguishes the newt from lizards. Adults hunt insects along canyon bottoms, and attract each other with odors transmitted through water. They breed underwater in stream pools and lay eggs on the stream

streams or ponds. Other reptiles also may be more abundant near moist sites, since prey insects and rodents are more plentiful there.

Because of its dangerous poison, the **southern Pacific rattlesnake** is the most feared and misunderstood reptile of the mountains (other poisonous snakes here include the **San Diego night snake** and the **lyre snake**, but these are seldom encountered and are not considered dangerous to humans). This snake, a subspecies of the western rattlesnake, averages four to five feet in length, is heavy-bodied,

Pacific treefrog

bottom; the eggs contain a paralyzing toxin that discourages most predators.

Reptiles are generally independent of water because their bodies are covered with scales or plates that protect them from injury and water loss. Also, their eggs are not as likely to dry out. Because reptiles are cold-blooded, they exist in a torpid state when temperatures are low.

Seven species of lizards, seventeen species of snakes, and one species of turtle occur in the mountains. The **western pond turtle**, **red-sided garter snake**, and the **two-striped garter snake** tend to prefer areas near

and has blotchy coloration. Like all rattlesnakes, it has a broad head with a pit below each eye; these pits serve as heat sensors to detect prey. During warmer months, you may encounter them along chaparral trails or in rocky areas. Rattlesnakes help keep rodent populations in check and are protected by law; do not molest them.

The white, black, and red or orange bands of the harmless **California mountain kingsnake** often lead people to mistake them for the poisonous coral snake, which is not found in this area. Kingsnakes kill their prey by constriction, and sometimes eat other snakes.

The **western fence lizard** and the **California side-blotched**

lizard, both ground-dwelling, are common throughout the mountains and feed mainly on insects. The **coast horned lizard** has a fierce-looking spiked head; a rough, spiky back; and habit of shooting blood from its eyes, all of which help deter attackers. It eats ants almost exclusively. The population of coast horned lizards is rapidly declining due to habitat loss. Other common lizards of the mountains include the coastal **whiptail lizard** and the **California** and **San Diego alligator lizards**.

Insects

In the winter, the **monarch butterfly** gathers in dense masses on certain trees in sheltered coastal canyons, having arrived from harsher climates farther north or inland. The bright orange color of the monarch warns potential predators to stay away, for while the monarch is in its caterpillar state, it feeds on the poisonous leaves of the milkweed, one of the few insects to do so, and this food source makes it a hazard to predators.

Stream ponds hold a wide array of unique and fascinating creatures, such as backswimmers, water striders, and creeping water bugs. Many periodically rise to the surface to trap air bubbles for use in stagnant, poorly oxygenated water. Most are predatory on other insects or even small amphibians and fish. A fearsome specimen is the **giant water bug**, otherwise—and perhaps more aptly—known as the "big toe biter." About one and one-half inches long, the giant water bug is the largest of the true bugs, and is a voracious predator.

Visitors to oak woodlands will find abundant evidence of one insect that is seldom seen itself. **Gall wasps** and **gall flies** lay eggs on oak branches, stimulating the tree to produce large (up to one and one-half inches), woody balls, sometimes called "oak apples."

Ticks are also common throughout the mountains, especially in the spring. Be sure to check yourself and your pet for ticks after a hike, and remove them carefully to prevent infection (see page 90).

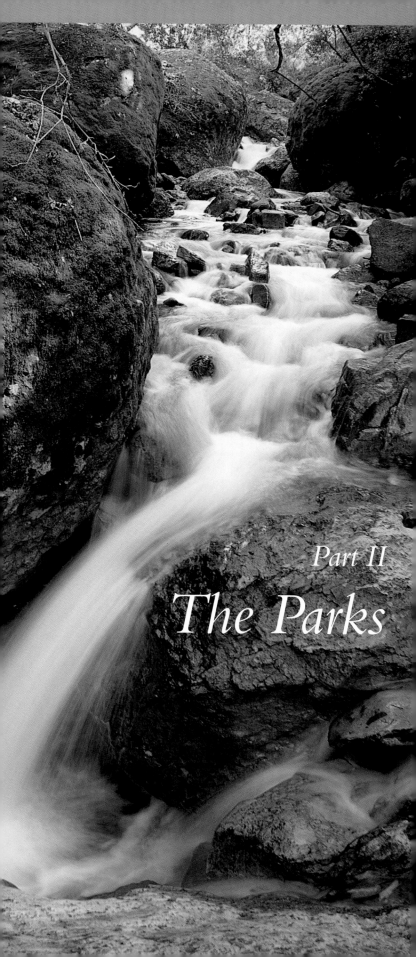

Part II
The Parks

Seabirds or spring wildflowers, old masters or musclemen, movie
sets or sand volleyball, surfing or hiking—all can be found in the
Santa Monica Mountains National Recreation Area.

Following is an alphabetical listing of the various recreation sites,
along with general information on each. In addition, the chart
on pages x to xii can help you find those areas that match your
particular interests. General information on trails and hikes is
included, but we recommend that you contact the area directly
for specifics such as degree-of-difficulty, parking areas for horse
trailers, and other relevant concerns. A contact phone number is
included in each entry—or, because status can change quickly, call
(800) 533-PARK for the most up-to-date information.

All of the parks can be reached by automobile, and some by
public transportation. Check with transit agencies for current
routes, schedules, and fees. Because parking is frequently limited,
public transportation (when available) is often more practical and
certainly more environmentally friendly. Call the Metropolitan
Transit Authority (MTA)/RTD at (310) 273-0910. To check for road
closures, call CalTrans at (800) 427-7623.

For information on surf conditions, call the Los Angeles County
Lifeguards at (310) 457-9701. Those concerned with accessibility
for the disabled should contact the area(s) directly for the most current information.

To make reservations for camping in the state parks, or for other
types of state park activity reservations, call MISTIX at (800) 444-
PARK (800-444-7275) within California, or (619) 425-1950 from
outside of California. (Various individual park listings will also refer
you to MISTIX.)

Photo previous page: Upper Sycamore Creek, Point Mugu State Park

1 Arroyo Sequit

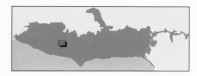

Location: Mulholland Highway, Malibu; see map page v

Administered by: National Park Service (818) 597-9192, ext. 201

Hours: Open twenty-four hours

Fees: No entrance fee

Facilities: Chemical toilets, picnic tables

Parking: Free but limited; parking lot open 8 A.M. to sunset daily

FYI: Dogs must be on leash. Firearms, bicycles, fires, and camping are prohibited.

A common pattern of settlement and development in the Santa Monica Mountains contradicts that seen in most of the country: here, the wealthy, not the agrarian poor, have traditionally been the first owners and settlers, buying isolated land as retreat homesites while working in the city and holding onto the land for speculation. That was the case at Arroyo Sequit where, in 1927, "gentleman farmer" Richard Mason and his family built a wood-frame house as a weekend home.

Today, the original ranch building is a staff residence.

You may park near the entrance on Mulholland Highway and stroll through the area's quiet grasslands mixed with chaparral, search the skies for hawks, and picnic under live oaks. In the meadows you can see traces of the old Decker Road, one of the pioneering roads through the Santa Monica Mountains.

Great horned owl

2 Castro Crest

Location: Corral Canyon Road, Malibu; see map page vi

Administered by: National Park Service (818) 597-9192, ext. 201

Hours: Open twenty-four hours

Fees: No entrance fee

Facilities: None

Parking: Free parking lot at end of Corral Canyon Road

FYI: Dogs must be on leash. Firearms, fires, and camping are prohibited.

The rugged fourteen hundred acres of public land at Castro Crest are some of the highest in

Castro Crest

the Santa Monica Mountains, over twenty-seven hundred feet above the sea. The park offers uncrowded hiking in an isolated terrain. The **Backbone Trail** bears left from the parking lot, down a south-facing chaparral slope with outstanding spring displays of wildflowers. The trail drops into a gentle valley and winds along upstream at the base

of a steep live oak-studded north slope along the way. At the head of the drainage, the trail passes through an area that burned in 1984. It switchbacks steeply to the drainage divide with Newton Canyon. The trail then descends the ridge to Latigo Canyon Road and on to Kanan Road.

Those who wish to climb to the lofty heights of Castro Crest should follow the **Castro Peak Motorway** out of the parking lot. This fire road follows the spine of the Santa Monica Mountains and provides incredible views of both the ocean and the inland valleys. Connecting to **Bulldog Motorway** for a twisting and precipitous descent into the backcountry of Malibu Creek State Park, this offers some of the best mountain bicycling in the Santa Monica Mountains.

3 Charmlee Natural Area

Location: Encinal Canyon Road, Malibu; see map page v

Administered by: City of Malibu (310) 457-7247

Hours: Sunrise to sunset

Fees: No entrance fee; fees for special facility rentals

Facilities: Restrooms, water, picnic tables, nature center

Parking: Paid off-street lots

FYI: Dogs must be on leash. Bicycles are discouraged but not prohibited. Alcohol, firearms, fires, and camping are prohibited.

Charmlee Natural Area is a fine mountain getaway at any time of the year. In the summer, cool sea breezes waft up the slopes from the foggy Malibu coast, the sun shines clear, and shade is abundant in the oak groves scattered throughout the park. Winter brings swirling mists and gentle rains alternating with crisp days and crystal-clear views of the ocean and Channel Islands. Spring harvests the bounty of winter rains in the form of a wild-flower extravaganza.

Called the *potrero* (meadow or corral) by early settlers, the park boasts an expanse of large grassy swards ringed by live oak-lined ravines and dotted with boulder-strewn islands of coastal sage scrub.

The walk-in picnic area in a grove of oaks is a great place for a family picnic, and here you'll be certain to find company (and possibly a bit of competition for meals) from abundant scrub jays. But better yet, take the forested **Botany Trail** or one of the several looping fire roads onto the grasslands and dine atop one of the many boulders in settings that resemble enchanted forests, with gnarled oaks overhanging.

At the southern end of the park, meadows give way to a line of bluffs with views of the coast. You may spot the tell-tale spouts of California gray whales during their annual migrations (December through February). In wet years, the bluffs and meadows are ablaze with outstanding wild-flower displays.

A nature center near the park's entrance has informational exhibits, a naturalist on duty on weekends to answer your questions, and displays of small live animals native to the park—snakes, birds, and amphibians. Volunteer naturalists lead the natural history tours for youth groups, weekend family nature hikes, monthly full-moon hikes, and school field trips.

4 Cheeseboro Canyon/ Palo Comado Canyon

Location: Chesebro Road, Agoura Hills; see map pages vi–vii

Administered by: National Park Service (818) 597-9192, ext. 201

Hours: Open twenty-four hours

Fees: No entrance fee

Facilities: Chemical toilets, picnic tables

Parking: Free NPS lot, open 8 A.M. to sunset

FYI: Dogs must be on leash. Firearms, fires, and camping are prohibited.

Peaceful Cheeseboro and Palo Comado canyons offer easy hiking, biking, and horseback riding in one of the finest examples of oak savanna remaining in southern California. The giant valley oaks—largest of the California oaks—spread their limbs over gentle, rolling grasslands that host deer, bobcats, coyotes, western gray squirrels, skunks, and a variety of predatory birds.

The area is a critical habitat linkage of fast-disappearing open space that connects the Santa Susana Mountain region to the north with the main Santa Monica Mountains area to the south. The habitat linkage allows animals to move between the two regions and permits the interbreeding so necessary to the maintenance of viable, adaptable populations.

The main trail up the canyon floor, the easy 4.6-mile **Cheeseboro Canyon Trail**, is an abandoned ranch road. It is wide and gentle.

The trail begins by passing through a grove of two- to three-hundred-year-old valley oaks, wildlife communities unto themselves. Hollow, rotten cores of the older trees are homes for ground squirrels, skunks, foxes, and other small animals; wild beehives also are common in such hollows. Ant trails reach to the heights of the great trees, where flycatchers and other birds nest. You are certain to hear the scolding cries of acorn woodpeckers, jaunty black-and-white birds with red caps, as they go about their business of perforating oak trunks for acorn stor-

Golden eagles have been sighted in Cheeseboro, and the cliffs are favored soaring territory for vultures as well as myriad birds of prey. The Santa Monica Mountains are home to more species of nesting raptors than anywhere else in the United States except the Snake River Birds of Prey National Conservation Area in Idaho.

The high, white cliffs of the Baleen Wall tower over the upper canyon and can be approached by

Coyote

age. Even in death, the trees serve: when they finally fall, their great skeletons of limbs and shattered trunks shelter and nourish a wealth of smaller animals and insects, and ultimately, the soil.

Virtually all grassland areas of southern California are missing a full generation of oaks, lost to the hordes of grazing animals beginning with the rancho period; you'll see mature oaks, but very few of young or intermediate age. The National Park Service is using livestock exclusion, prescribed fires, seeding, and other techniques to ensure that the great oaks and other components of the Santa Monica Mountains ecosystem persist.

the 3-mile **Baleen Wall Trail**, which forms a loop (closed to bicycles) off the **Cheeseboro Canyon Trail.**

Another possible loop back to the trailhead is the .75-mile **Modelo Trail**, which climbs the west ridge of the canyon and allows you a look into neighboring Agoura Hills. This trail serves as a link to Palo Comado Canyon.

The main **Palo Comado Trail** travels over a service road the length of the canyon to China Flat. This grassland, with oaks and rock outcroppings, is a great picnic spot. Above China Flat is 2,403-foot Simi Peak. On a clear day the view of the surrounding area is spectacular.

5 Circle X Ranch

Location: Yerba Buena Road, Malibu; see map page v

Administered by: National Park Service (818) 597-9192, ext. 201, or Circle X Ranger Station (310) 457-6408

Hours: Open twenty-four hours

Fees: No entrance fee. Fee for camping. Ranch house use fee

Facilities: Camp grounds, chemical toilets; detailed information in entry

Parking: Four free NPS lots, one at the ranger station and three on Yerba Buena Road

FYI: Bicycles allowed only on the portion of Backbone Trail to Split Rock Trail. Dogs must be on leash, and are not allowed on state park property. Firearms, open fires, and motor vehicles on trails and fire roads are prohibited.

The parklands of Circle X Ranch embrace 3,111-foot Sandstone Peak—the highest point in the Santa Monica Mountains—and are perhaps the best-kept secret in the national recreation area. In the quiet heights of upper Arroyo Sequit, the park offers camping, hiking, riding, and backpacking, as well as group-use facilities.

In 1946, members of the Exchange Club, a service and social club of businessmen, resolved to establish a "ranch" to which youth groups of all types could come to camp and learn self-reliance. After a year's search, they purchased the 160-acre home of Donald Crisp, star of *How Green Was My Valley* (filmed at Malibu Creek State Park), in the farthest, highest corner of the Santa Monica Mountains for twenty-five thousand dollars. The nonprofit Circle X Ranch Foundation was formed to buy and administer the ranch; the name was taken from the Exchange Club's emblem.

The club enlisted the aid of the Navy Seabees construction battalion from nearby Port Hueneme. As a part of unit training, the Seabees built water tanks and pipe systems, cut firebreaks and roads, leveled camping areas, and cleared brush.

In 1949, the club successfully completed negotiations to make Circle X a camp exclusively for the use of the Boy Scouts of America. Working together over the next six years, the Boy Scouts and Circle X directors acquired an additional 1,561 acres of deep canyons, brushy hillsides, and the ramparts of Sandstone Peak, and enlarged facilities to handle a thousand scouts. A disastrous fire in 1955 and another in 1956 only redoubled the devotees' drive to make Circle X a first-class camp. Seabees, club volunteers, and scouts worked to reforest burned slopes, establish new water sources, improve campsites, and build new facilities. The property was finally sold to the State of California, from whom the National Park Service purchased it in 1989.

Trails: From the Group Campground, the **Grotto Trail** descends steeply down a chaparral slope 1.7 miles to Happy Hollow Campground. It's a dizzying look down the sheer cascade and an inspiring view of the stony ridges across the wilds of upper Arroyo Sequit. Small meadows along the trail show off popcorn flowers, brodiaea species, phacelia, and mariposa lilies in the spring. Vines of giant, spiny, wild cucumbers clamber over ceanothus bushes. Below the campground, the stream has water in it most of the year, and the trail soon becomes a rocky scramble. The Grotto itself,

Golden eagle

just south of the Happy Hollow Campground, is a cavelike maze, with waterfalls and deep pools inaccessible beneath house-sized chunks of volcanic *breccia* (rock made up of melded angular fragments of older rocks) that have *spalled* (chipped) off the sheer rock walls above.

Views are good and the grade is moderate on the 1.4-mile **Canyon View Trail**, which stretches between the hiker parking lot and the Backbone Trail parking lot, one mile east of the ranger station on Yerba Buena Road.

The 1.2-mile route to the peak up the **Backbone Trail** from the parking lot follows a graded fire road. On clear days, the short, steep, final scramble to the summit will reward you with top-of-the-world views of the wild western portion of the mountains and the Channel Islands. While on top, be sure to scan the skies for the rare golden eagles and peregrine falcons known to frequent these heights. Also note the

13-million-year-old volcanic rocks that make up this and surrounding peaks—"Sandstone Peak" is a misnomer.

Perhaps the best opportunity for long-distance hiking in these mountains is from here at Sandstone Peak to Rancho Sierra Vista through Point Mugu State Park.

The chaparral here, as around all of Sandstone Peak, has conspicuous stands of red shank bushes. These tall, feathery shrubs with reddish-brown shredded bark are otherwise found only in the area between Santa Cruz, California, and northern Baja California. Red shank, also called ribbonwood, is closely related to chamise but is a much taller (up to twenty feet) shrub that tends to grow in moister sites. Strings of red bark hang off the trunk and leaves are small and needlelike but are not in clumps as are those of chamise. Red shank occurs in a few noncontiguous populations in the state. In the Santa Monica Mountains, it grows around

Circle X Ranch, Cold Creek, Saddle Peak, and Zuma Ridge.

From the camp, the **Backbone Trail** branches west into the Boney Mountain State Wilderness, but many hikers turn north and east to complete a six-mile loop down the **Mishe Mokwa Trail**. The trail drops into a long, deep valley between impressive cliffs on the densely forested Sandstone Peak and Conejo Peak. Deep in the canyon forest is famous Split Rock, a giant boulder of volcanic breccia cleaved into three pieces with just room enough to walk through, an ideal rest stop with shade, picnic tables, and an intermittent stream.

Soon, spectacular views of the cliffs at the head of Carlisle Canyon and a giant balanced rock on the top come into sight. Rock slopes here nourish verdant gardens of club moss and succulent live-forever. Downhill, you'll pass through chaparral, with chamise, red shank, and laurel sumac dominating. The Mishe Mokwa Trail intersects with the Backbone Trail fire road about .3 mile from the Backbone Trail parking lot.

Picnicking, camping, and group use facilities: A small picnic area is nestled into the creekside forest just below the ranger station, off Yerba Buena Road.

All campsites at **Happy Hollow Campground** (elevation 1,100 feet) require a short walk across the creek from the parking areas and are restricted to tenters. Reservations are not accepted, but call ahead to be sure the camp is open; rain can cause it to be closed during certain months. The solitude at Happy Hollow, privacy from other campsites, and the quiet location away from all roads make camping here unique.

Sites are scattered through a beautiful streamside setting. Facilities date from Boy Scout days—part of the camp's appeal to the Boy Scouts was the 1,100-foot elevation, which gave them opportunities for a grueling training hike to Sandstone Peak, a climb of two thousand feet in three miles. A short walk below the camp is the Grotto. Along the way, you'll find deep pools with frogs and newts and perhaps a smattering of wildflowers such as shooting stars.

Campsites are available on a first-come, first-served basis; there is self-registration and a fee is charged; Golden Age and Golden Access passports apply. This is a tents-only area; vehicles over twenty-five feet and trailers are prohibited. Sites are limited to six persons, two tents, and two vehicles. All vehicles are prohibited in campsites—park and walk across the bridge. Dogs on leash are permitted; water, picnic tables, pit toilets are provided; and propane stoves and charcoal fires can be used in the installed braziers. The campground is closed in winter months; call the park service offices at (818) 597-9192, ext. 201 to verify availability.

At a 1,600-foot elevation and close to Yerba Buena Road is the **group campground**, the original Circle X campsite. There is a limit

Shooting star

of fifty persons per group and the site is available by reservation only, up to three months in advance; call (310) 457-6408 and leave a message; a ranger will return your call. A fee is charged; Golden Age and Golden Access passports do not apply. Water, picnic tables, and pit toilets are available and gas stoves and charcoal fires are permitted in the installed braziers. Dogs are also permitted, on-leash only.

The **ranch house** is available for meetings or other events. There are kitchen and shower facilities, but no overnight stays can be accommodated. The capacity is seventy-five people and it is available by special use permit (a fee is charged); call (310) 457-6408 for information and reservations.

6 Cold Creek Canyon Preserve

Location: Stunt Road, Malibu; see map page vii

Administered by: Mountains Restoration Trust (310) 456-5625

Hours: Sunrise to sunset, by reservation only. Call ahead for permit

Fees: No entrance fee

Facilities: None

Parking: Limited on-road parking

FYI: Advance reservations are required for entry. Alcohol, firearms, motor vehicles, bicycles, fires, camping, dogs, and horses are prohibited.

Cold Creek Canyon Preserve is an ecological treasure, showcasing a wider variety of native plants and animals in its compact seven hundred acres than any other similar-size area in the Santa Monica Mountains. Cold Creek has its headwaters here, rising from springs in a cool, moist, north-facing basin studded with giant sandstone boulders and cliffs. The water is of such purity that it is used as a benchmark for measuring degradation in other Santa Monica Mountains streams.

A 1.6-mile trail descends the shaded north slope from Stunt Road near Saddle Peak to the lower gate near the falls. It alternately passes

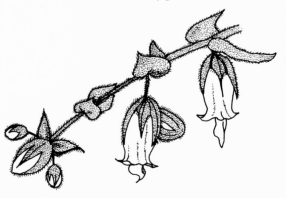

Pitcher sage

through mixed chaparral and sun-dappled oak forests with an occasional breakout into a hot and dry section of coastal sage scrub. Good flower displays can be expected from March through September.

Deeper in the canyon, "weeping" boulders at seeps harbor gardens of ferns. The red flower spikes of the pitcher sage can be seen in openings near oaks and bays. Along the banks of Cold Creek, in a riparian woodland, big-leaf maples, California bay trees, sycamores, and coast live oaks arch over the stream. All of the preserve is rich in wildlife, but the riparian woodland is especially so, with gray fox, ringtails, raccoons, and bobcats occupying territories in this area.

Part way down, you will see the remains of the unique home of Herman Hethke. This German immigrant homesteaded Cold Creek in the early 1900s and built his home in the giant sandstone boulders. Hethke blasted the interior and doorway and installed a porch and corrugated tin roof. The celery he planted in the adjacent bog has gone wild and can be seen today, mixed with sedges and ferns.

Because Cold Creek Canyon Preserve is a remnant of an ecosystem beseiged by urban development and is intended as a refuge for rare and sensitive plants and animals, access is limited to twenty-five persons per day and advance reservations for entry are required. Guided nature walks are periodically led by the Cold Creek Docents. The Mountains Restoration Trust sponsors interpretive walks the second Saturday of each month; subjects range from geology to fungi.

7 Cold Creek Valley Preserve

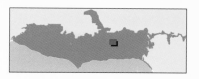

Location: Stunt Road, Malibu; see map page vii

Administered by: Mountains Restoration Trust
(310) 456-5625

Hours: Sunrise to sunset

Fees: No entrance fee

Facilities: None

Parking: Free at Stunt High Trail or along road

FYI: Alcohol, firearms, motor vehicles, bicycles, fires, camping, dogs, and horses are prohibited.

Cold Creek Valley Preserve, south of Stunt Ranch, is framed by the sandstone plates that make up the sides of the Cold Creek "bowl"; both this area and Cold Creek Canyon Preserve are in the Cold Creek Watershed. Life is everywhere here: red-shouldered hawks and turkey vultures soar, rufous and brown towhees jump-scratch for grubs, colorful wildflowers bloom after winter rains. The soft sand holds tracks of coyotes, bobcats, lizards, and snakes as well as of many small birds. Microclimates encourage and shelter special plants. Altogether, this small, fifty-six-acre area gives you a sense of serenity as you walk its trails and observe its inhabitants.

8 Coldwater Canyon Park

Location: Coldwater Canyon Drive, Beverly Hills; see map page ix

Administered by: TreePeople (818) 753-4600

Hours: Sunrise to sunset

Fees: No entrance fee; nominal fee for trail guide

Facilities: Restrooms, water, picnic tables

Parking: Free off-street lot; parking lot opens at 9 A.M

FYI: Dogs must be on leash. Alcohol, smoking, firearms, bicycles, fires, barbecues, camping, and horses are prohibited.

Formerly the mountain-patrol headquarters for the Los Angeles Fire Department, Coldwater Canyon Park is now an environmental education center operated by TreePeople. It has seven miles of nature trails and many environmentally focused displays. Reservations may be made for guided Sunday tours by calling (818) 753-4608. The park is a great destination for school field trips.

9 Corral Canyon/Dan Blocker State Beach

Location: Pacific Coast Highway, Malibu; see map page vi

Administered by: Los Angeles County Beaches and Harbors (310) 305-9503

Hours: Sunrise to 10 P.M.

Fees: No entrance fee

Facilities: Chemical toilets, food concessions

Parking: Free off-street parking on Pacific Coast Highway

FYI: Alcohol, firearms, bicycles, fires, camping, dogs, and horses are prohibited.

Corral Canyon/Dan Blocker State Beach is a narrow beach beside Pacific Coast Highway, popular for sunbathing, surf fishing, and swimming (although the bottom is rocky). Spring displays of exotic yellow mustard on hillsides above are spectacular. Hikers can take advantage of the beach's location at the mouth of Solstice Canyon by following the creekbed upstream for an ocean-to-mountains experience.

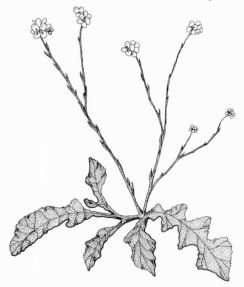

Yellow mustard

10 El Matador State Beach

Location: Pacific Coast Highway, Malibu; see map page v

Administered by: California Department of Parks and Recreation (818) 880-0350

Hours: 8 A.M. to sunset

Fees: No entrance fee

Facilities: Chemical toilets, water, picnic tables

Parking: Paid parking lot off Pacific Coast Highway

FYI: Tidepools here, but no lifeguard service. Downhill walk to the beach via stairs. Dogs must be on leash. Alcohol, firearms, bicycles, camping, and horses are prohibited.

Scenic El Matador State Beach encompasses a surprisingly wide range of features and environments within its eighteen acres. The blufftop picnic area affords excellent views of the ocean and shoreline kelp beds. Stands of wind- and salt-sheared laurel sumac give way to steep cliffs dotted with yucca, cacti, giant coreopsis, and lemonadeberry. At the end of the .8-mile trail and staircase to the narrow beach, waves often lap right at the base of the cliffs at high tide and prevent the formation of the unusual transitional plant community known as coastal strand. This same steep terrain has a series of dramatic caves and arches in detached rocks, home to barnacles, anemones, and mussels (visible at low tide). They are also favorite perches for pelicans, cormorants, and other sea birds.

El Matador offers secluded sunbathing and swimming (no lifeguard service), scuba diving, good surf fishing, and places to forget the bustle of the city so nearby.

11 El Pescador State Beach

Location: Pacific Coast Highway, Malibu; see map page v

Administered by: California Department of Parks and Recreation (818) 880-0350

Hours: 8 A.M. to sunset

Fees: No entrance fee

Facilities: Chemical toilets, picnic tables

Parking: Paid parking

FYI: Downhill walk to the beach via stairs. Dogs must be on leash at all times. Alcohol, firearms, bicycles, fires, camping, and horses are prohibited.

El Pescador State Beach is a tiny (nine-acre) "pocket beach," a quiet and intimate setting for sunbathing, picnicking, and fishing. Rip currents frequently occur here, and no lifeguard service is provided.

At low tide, starfish, sea anemones, clams, periwinkles, and shrimp may be seen in the cobbled pools below the beach line. Up the trail on the cliff top, picnic tables are provided in a grassy field that in the spring is covered by exotic yellow mustard.

Brown pelican

12 Franklin Canyon Ranch

Location: Lake Drive, Beverly Hills; see map page ix

Administered by: National Park Service (818) 597-9192, ext. 201

Hours: Open twenty-four hours

Fees: No entrance fee; permits and fees required for groups

Facilities: Restrooms, water, limited picnic areas

Parking: Limited free street and NPS lot parking; lots open 8 A.M. to sunset. Not recommended for buses

FYI: Bicycles and horses restricted to specific use areas. Dogs must be on leash. Firearms, fires, and camping are prohibited.

At Franklin Canyon Ranch, hidden at the bottom of a deep valley in the mountains of Beverly Hills, you can easily forget that you are surrounded by an ocean of clamoring city. That in fact was the hope of one of the canyon's former owners, Edward L. Doheny, who bought the site in 1912 as part of a four hundred-acre parcel. Today, the ranch is publicly held, an oasis in this otherwise exclusive urban area.

Instrumental in locating oil fields in the Los Angeles area, Doheny made his fortune selling oil to the Southern Pacific Railroad. In 1935, he built an elegantly simple Spanish-style stucco house at the site. While he was not interested in commercial ranching, he did keep the land open, and subsequent owners stocked it with longhorns, zebras, antelope, peacocks, and ostriches. Today these animals are gone, leaving the steep, chaparral-covered canyon slopes and canyon-bottom woodlands of live oak, black walnut, and sycamore to the native coyotes, deer, and smaller animals.

A broad lawn below the ranch house is shaded by sycamore and flowering jacaranda trees and is an ideal site for small outdoor weddings or parties (reserve the site in advance for group activities), or simply as a place for the family to relax. Volunteers from the nearby William O. Douglas Outdoor Classroom give nature programs at a small amphitheater here, and lead walks along three nature trails through the valley and up the canyon slopes. One of the most popular is a moonlight hike up the wide, 1.8-mile **Hastain Trail** for spectacular views of surrounding Los Angeles to the coast. Other trails

Mule deer

include the .3-mile self-guided **Discovery Trail** and the .4-mile **Sycamore Loop Trail**.

Groups larger than fifty must notify National Park Service staff so that conflict with other groups is avoided. Fee permits are required for organized groups, amplified music, or games. Bicycles and horses are permitted only on Lake Drive and the fire road section of the Hastain Trail.

13 Fryman Canyon

Location: Mulholland Drive, Beverly Hills; see map page ix

Administered by: Santa Monica Mountains Conservancy
(310) 456-5046
(800) 533-PARK

Hours: 8 A.M. to 5 P.M.

Fees: No entrance fee

Facilities: Water, limited number of picnic tables, fitness stations

Parking: Extremely limited street parking

FYI: No restrooms available at this site. Dogs must be on leash. Alcohol, firearms, bicycles, fires, camping, and horses are prohibited.

Fryman Canyon, a wooded area with a small spring, can be hiked into from Wilacre Park or Coldwater Canyon Park. The wayside overlook on Mulholland Drive provides views of the San Fernando Valley, Santa Susana Mountains, and the west end of the San Gabriel Mountains. You can also take the **Betty B. Dearing Mountain Trail**, which begins at the overlook, and traverse steep chaparral slopes to Coldwater Canyon Park and on to Wilacre Park.

14 J. Paul Getty Museum

Location: 17985 Pacific Coast Highway, Malibu; see map page viii

Administered by: The J. Paul Getty Trust
(310) 458-2003, or
TDD for hearing-impaired
(310) 394-7448

Hours: 10 A.M. to 5 P.M., Tuesday through Sunday; closed Mondays and major holidays

Fees: No entrance fee; pass required

Facilities: Restroom

Parking: No parking fee is charged but advance parking reservations are required; call ahead.

FYI: All galleries and most facilities are wheelchair-accessible. Picnic lunches, bare feet, beach attire, and cleated shoes are prohibited.

Los Angeles residents oppressed by the bustle of twentieth-century living can find respite on their doorstep at the J. Paul Getty Museum in Malibu. Getty was an internationally known billionaire oil tycoon with a passion for collecting the finest of the fine arts. Following Getty's death in 1982, most of his estate passed to the J. Paul Getty Trust, which now sponsors its own programs and grants, promoting public education in the visual arts and related humanities.

The museum building is patterned after several Roman structures, but especially the first century A.D. Roman country house, Villa dei Papiri. Outside the museum are five formal gardens planted with herbs, shrubs, vines, and trees that reflect the Mediterranean environment of two thousand years ago and bespeak the significance of gardens to Romans, as both spiritual and practical sources of comfort, food, and medicines. Inside the museum, you will find major permanent collections of Greek and Roman antiquities. The painting collection includes masterworks by Renoir, van Gogh, Munch, Pontormo, Rembrandt, and others. Work by da Vinci, Raphael, van Dyck, Dürer, Watteau, Goya, Cézanne, and van Gogh grace the collection of drawings; and Georg Hoefnagel, Jean Fouquet, Taddeo Crivelli, and Simon Bening are stars of the collection of European and Byzantine illuminated manuscripts. The European sculpture collection from the Middle Ages to the late nineteenth century includes works by Bernini, Giambologna, de Vries, Carpeaux, and Antico. Seventeenth- to early nineteenth-century royal French decorative arts are exhibited in rooms recreated to reflect this period. The museum has recently taken a strong interest in acquiring European and American photographs dating from the early 1840s through the 1950s, and displays works by Talbot, Cameron, Nadar, Cunningham, Kertesz, Strand, Sander, and Weston, among others.

In addition to rotating displays of the museum's permanent art collection, the Getty also offers visiting exhibitions, a lecture series, art history classes, family programs, a concert series, and books and audiovisual materials on its various collections. There is a bookstore and garden tea room. Evening lectures are free, but reservations are required. Summer concert series tickets are sold through Ticketmaster at (213) 480-3232.

For school groups, lessons and pre-visit materials are available at no charge; call (310) 459-7611. Gallery talks or seminars may be arranged six weeks in advance for groups affiliated with art or academic institutions; call (310) 459-7611.

15 La Piedra State Beach

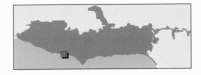

Location: Pacific Coast Highway, Malibu; see map page v

Administered by: California Department of Parks and Recreation (818) 880-0350

Hours: 8 A.M. to sunset

Fees: No entrance fee

Facilities: Chemical toilets, water, picnic tables

Parking: Paid parking

FYI: No lifeguard service here. Dogs must be on leash at all times. Alcohol, fires, camping, and horses are prohibited.

La Piedra State Beach is a "pocket beach," tiny, secluded, and surrounded by private property. This is one of three local beaches (along with El Pescador and El Matador) designated as the Robert H. Meyer Memorial State Beaches in honor of Mr. Meyer's work to provide public parks and recreation areas close to populated areas.

The beach here is short, very narrow, cobbled, and completely swallowed by waves at high tide. Still, it offers a refreshing picnic site and sunbathing away from crowds. Tidepool study, scuba diving, and surfing are among the other activities popular here. Along the trail up a narrow draw to the blufftop picnic tables, you can see cliffside flora of purple sage, bladderpod, giant coreopsis, laurel sumac, canyon sunflower, and exotic ice plant and mustards.

16 Las Tunas State Beach

Location: Pacific Coast Highway, Malibu; see map page vii

Administered by: Los Angeles County Beaches and Harbors
(310) 305-9503

Hours: Sunrise to 10 P.M.

Fees: No entrance fee

Facilities: Chemical toilet

Parking: Limited free street parking on Pacific Coast Highway

FYI: Alcohol, firearms, motor vehicles, bicycles, fires, camping, dogs, and horses are prohibited.

"Las Tunas" refers not to the fish, but to the Spanish name for the prickly pear cactus, which grows in abundance on hillsides above this narrow beach immediately beside Pacific Coast Highway. Sunbathing and swimming are allowed, but the beach is rocky and may almost disappear at high tide. The beach is better known for its fishing, with California corbina and barred surf perch most commonly caught. Offshore is a rocky reef occasionally visited by divers.

17 Laurel Canyon Park

Location: Mulholland Drive, Studio City; see map page ix

Administered by: Los Angeles City Department of Recreation and Parks
(818) 756-8891

Hours: 5 A.M. to 10:30 P.M.

Fees: No entrance fee

Facilities: Restrooms, water, picnic tables, children's play area

Parking: Free but limited off-street parking

FYI: An urban "dog park"! Dogs allowed off leash between 7 A.M. and 10 A.M., 3 P.M. to closing, and on-leash at any time. Alcohol, firearms, motor vehicles, bicycles, fires, camping, and horses are prohibited.

Shade trees and a playground are two attractions at Laurel Canyon Park, a flat, grassy area in the midst of chaparral hillsides and suburban housing developments. But the main draw is the dog action. The park is "dog city," a pilot project of the City of Los Angeles that provides an area where dogs are welcome any time and can run free during certain hours. During the "off-leash" hours especially, the park is awash with hundreds of dogs of every description, cavorting in harmony. To help make this project a success, observe leash restriction hours and be sure to clean up after your dog.

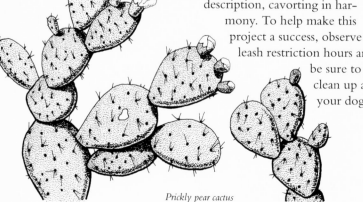

Prickly pear cactus

18 Leo Carrillo State Beach

Location: Pacific Coast Highway, Malibu; see map page v

Administered by: California Department of Parks and Recreation (805) 986-8591

Hours: Open twenty-four hours

Fees: No entrance fee; fee for overnight camping

Facilities: Flush- and chemical toilets, water, picnic tables, camping

Parking: Day-use paid parking lot (8 A.M. to sunset)

FYI: Dogs are permitted on beaches except between towers two and three. Motor vehicles are restricted. Smoking during high fire-hazard seasons, firearms, bicycles, fires, and horses are prohibited.

With more than a mile of quiet beaches and rocky headlands known for their beauty, three campgrounds, and two thousand acres of mountainous backcountry, Leo Carrillo State Beach is one of the most diverse and popular park sites easily accessible to Los Angeles and Ventura County residents. The park is named for the actor Leo Carrillo (sidekick Pancho in the television show *The Cisco Kid*), honoring his work to acquire this and other beachfront properties for public use. The park's association with the motion picture industry continues today, as much filming goes on here. Sequit Point divides North Beach from South Beach.

Leo Carrillo is one of the primary surfing areas along the Los Angeles coast, and windy exposure at the cobble-strewn east end of South Beach draws windsurfers from throughout southern California. With the extensive kelp beds nearby, varied seafloor, and protected beach entry, Leo Carrillo is also the most frequented area for scuba diving north of Marina Del Rey. The water here is so clean that in 1969, it was used as a nonpolluted comparison site for studying the effects of the disastrous Santa Barbara oil spill.

The sheltered, pure sand expanse of South Beach is a favorite with families, and the small estuary of Arroyo Sequit is a perfect place for small children to splash. Two ocean-carved arches and a tunnel pass completely through the westernmost of the three points of adjacent Sequit Point. Tiny pocket beaches in between offer privacy and shelter for picnicking or sunbathing on a windy day.

Rocky tidepools at the point hide a host of fascinating creatures such as sea anemones, hermit crabs, limpets, chitons, starfish, sea slugs, and an occasional octopus. Most of these creatures are especially adapted to the intertidal zone, the area between high and low tides. The best viewing opportunities are at low tides; a tide book or a park ranger can help you determine when these occur. Intertidal zones may dry out completely at low tide or be exposed to higher doses of damaging solar radiation than areas in deeper water. Tidepool ecosystems throughout the state, but especially in southern California, are in extreme danger from careless or deliberately destructive visitors. Do not remove tidepool creatures or turn them over; in addition, do not turn over the rocks or shells that shelter them.

Starfish

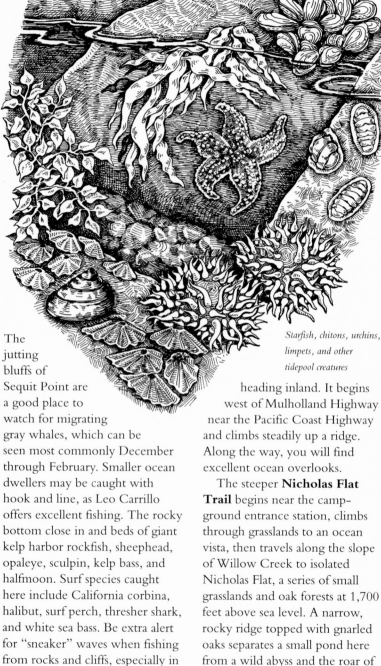

Starfish, chitons, urchins, limpets, and other tidepool creatures

The jutting bluffs of Sequit Point are a good place to watch for migrating gray whales, which can be seen most commonly December through February. Smaller ocean dwellers may be caught with hook and line, as Leo Carrillo offers excellent fishing. The rocky bottom close in and beds of giant kelp harbor rockfish, sheephead, opaleye, sculpin, kelp bass, and halfmoon. Surf species caught here include California corbina, halibut, surf perch, thresher shark, and white sea bass. Be extra alert for "sneaker" waves when fishing from rocks and cliffs, especially in winter.

Much of the park's interior consists of steep chaparral-covered hillsides sliced by intermittent streams lined with lush growths of willows, California bay trees (sometimes called myrtlewood), sycamores, black walnut, and scattered live oaks.

The **Yellow Hill Trail** is the easier of the two main trails heading inland. It begins west of Mulholland Highway near the Pacific Coast Highway and climbs steadily up a ridge. Along the way, you will find excellent ocean overlooks.

The steeper **Nicholas Flat Trail** begins near the campground entrance station, climbs through grasslands to an ocean vista, then travels along the slope of Willow Creek to isolated Nicholas Flat, a series of small grasslands and oak forests at 1,700 feet above sea level. A narrow, rocky ridge topped with gnarled oaks separates a small pond here from a wild abyss and the roar of the Pacific below. Birdwatching along the shore and adjoining forest and grasslands is excellent, and there is a surprising abundance of toads and frogs here in a wet spring.

Camping: Many a Los Angeles child has had his or her first camping experience at Leo Carrillo State Beach. Its proximity to the city brings diverse groups, and the varied environment, from the ocean to the mountains, offers a rich experience.

Although windy and exposed, **North Beach Campground** allows campers with recreational vehicles the rare opportunity to camp right next to the beach. This is the perfect takeoff place for surfers, surf fishers, and families spending a lazy day on the sand. Camping specifics: thirty-two sites, self-contained RVs only; no hookups. No tents allowed. Water, picnic tables, charcoal stoves, restrooms, cold showers. Interpretive exhibits in season. Make reservations through MISTIX, (800) 444-PARK.

Canyon Campground affords family camping at its best. Located near the mouth of Arroyo Sequit, on the site of what was a Chumash village, the campground is nestled in a lush *riparian* (streamside) grove of large elderberry bushes and giant sycamore trees, some of which have a spread of more than a hundred feet. Campers enjoy nature, exploring along the creek as it reaches deep into the mountains, and in the chaparral and quiet grasslands of the hillsides. Camping specifics: 138 sites for tents and RVs up to thirty-one feet; no hookups. Limit eight persons per site. One campsite designated for people traveling by foot or bicycle. Water, picnic tables, charcoal stoves, restrooms, hot showers, sanitary dump station, camp store. Reserve through MISTIX, (800) 444-PARK.

A **walk-in group campground** is located at the upper end of Canyon Campground; it can accommodate up to fifty people. Camping specifics: water, picnic tables, barbecue pits, restrooms, hot showers; available by reservation only. Reserve through MISTIX, (800) 444-PARK.

Nature walks and evening campfire programs are given seasonally by park rangers and an amphitheater is located at the upper end of Canyon Campground.

19 Malibu Bluffs

Location: Pacific Coast Highway, Malibu; see map page vii
Administered by: City of Malibu (310) 317-1364
Hours: 9 A.M. to sunset
Fees: No entrance fee. Rental fees for park and indoor facility
Facilities: Restrooms, water, picnic tables, two baseball diamonds, soccer field, Michael Landon Community Center
Parking: Free parking lot
FYI: Dogs are permitted on leash only. Alcohol, firearms, motor vehicles, bicycles, fires, camping, and horses are prohibited.

Malibu Bluffs, at the junction of Malibu Canyon Road and the Pacific Coast Highway below Pepperdine University, is the home for area Little League baseball teams. Spacious lawns offer soccer fields and three baseball diamonds. Paved walkways line the periphery, with picnic tables and fitness stations interspersed. A stairway down the bluff to the beach passes a large, grassy meadow, a great place for kite flying and picnicking. From the bluffs, you can see all of Santa Monica Bay in one sweep. To the southwest, Santa Barbara Island can be seen on a clear day, and southeast is the famous Santa Catalina Island.

20 Malibu Creek State Park

Location: Las Virgenes Road, Calabasas; see map page vi

Administered by: California Department of Parks and Recreation (818) 880-0367

Hours: Open twenty-four hours

Fees: Parking fee is day use fee; fee for overnight camping

Facilities: Restrooms, water, picnic tables, group picnic area

Parking: Paid off-street lot

FYI: Bicycles are restricted to fire roads. Dogs must be on leash and are not allowed on trails. Alcohol, firearms, ground fires, and wood collecting are prohibited.

An astonishing array of features is packed into the seven thousand acres of Malibu Creek State Park, a land rich in modern history and ancient geologic turmoil. Hiking, biking, or horseback riding on one or more of the park's twenty trails will get you into the interior, where you'll find hidden waterfalls and a lake, sheer rocky cliffs, streamside forests, broad meadows, and pastoral oak woodlands. Mountains and isolated buttes that reveal the volcanic and marine origins of this land are deeply cleft by canyons and valleys, affording the illusion of being in a vast and remote wilderness. The park offers one of the few opportunities in the Santa Monica Mountains for freshwater fishing and swimming as well as the closest campground to the L.A. metropolitan area. For decades, the varied terrain has been a draw to the motion picture industry.

Naturalist walks are regularly scheduled throughout the year, and reservations can be made for group programs. Three areas in the park have been designated as natural preserves to better protect rare botanical and geological treasures and a varied wildlife population, which includes mountain lions, golden eagles, bobcats, mule deer, badgers, red-shouldered and red-tailed hawks, and a host of smaller animals.

Although the Chumash lived here for thousands of years, taking advantage of year-round water and an abundant acorn supply, they left few traces. The **Talepop Trail** in the northeast portion of the park is named for a small Chumash village.

In 1853, prominent area rancher Don Pedro Alcantara Sepulveda built the Sepulveda Adobe near Las Virgenes Creek. This oldest European structure in the mountains still stands along the Talepop Trail just north of Mulholland Highway (walls are shorn up with protective sheathing, pending restoration). One visitor to the Sepulveda Adobe may have been the infamous bandit Joaquin Murietta, whose band was said to hide out at a giant seven hundred-year-old oak in preparation for heists along El Camino Real, a few miles to the north. The oak can still be seen, now fallen at the base of Mendenhall Canyon.

A series of American homesteaders occupied the land through the end of the 1800s, farming, raising grapes and goats, and selling charcoal made from the giant oaks. The last of the settlers were a group of wealthy businessmen who in 1900 formed the Crags Country Club. They worked communally to become self-sufficient, raising beef and dairy cattle, hogs, poultry, fruit, and hay. The current visitor center (Hunter House) was one of the original country club homes.

(continued on page 50)

A Modern History of Malibu

El Rancho Topanga Malibu Sequit was the last of the major Mexican land grants in southern California to be subdivided, a holdout until the 1920s and 1930s from the great American urban sprawl. This thin, twenty-three-mile stretch of the Malibu coastline—from Santa Monica to the Oxnard Plain, from ocean to mountain crest—remains relatively undeveloped.

The Spaniard José Bartolomé Tapia was a member of the 1773 overland expedition of Juan Bautista de Anza. In about 1842, he became the first European "owner" of the Malibu, having been granted grazing and occupancy rights to the land by the Spanish commander of the military garrison in Santa Barbara.

Tapia built an adobe home in Malibu Canyon, raised grapes, and herded six thousand head of cattle in this remote, roadless rancho. After Mexico's independence from Spain was declared in 1822, his heirs attempted to secure a Mexican land grant but were unsuccessful in proving their claim to the land. Nevertheless, the Tapia family retained tenancy to the Malibu, and in 1848—on the day gold was discovered in northern California —José Bartolomé's wife sold Rancho Malibu to her son-in-law Leon Victor Prudhomme and her daughter María Merced Tapia for a mere four hundred pesos. Prudhomme's subsequent claim to a valid land grant was denied by the new United States Land Commission. Discouraged by both his legal defeat and declining cattle prices, Prudhomme sold any interest he legally had in the ranch to an Irish land speculator, Matthew

Keller, in 1857 for $1,400, about ten cents an acre.

Early on, Keller had planted vineyards and oranges in the L.A. area and was a cofounder of the Pioneer Oil Company and the Los Angeles & San Pedro Railroad. He constructed ranch buildings in Zuma Canyon and a rock home in Solstice Canyon, the oldest non-Spanish structure still standing in the national recreation area *(see Solstice Canyon listing)*. Keller succeeded where others failed, and managed to convince the land commission to confirm his claim and convey a patent to the land. This claim began at the ocean and ran about one mile inland, and from Las Flores Canyon to Arroyo Sequit—approximately 13,300 acres in all. This was still only about one-third the area of the original Tapia land concession; the remaining portions, mostly inland, were declared government land and later homesteaded by others.

In 1892, Frederick Hastings Rindge and May K. Rindge became the last private individuals to own the bulk of the Rancho Malibu as a single unit. They bought it from Keller's heirs for ten dollars an acre, and later expanded it to seventeen thousand acres. Heir to a fortune made in the wool trade, Frederick Rindge was a philanthropist, a leader in the temperance movement and local government, and vice-president of the Union Oil Company. He and May moved to Santa Monica from Boston, having found the paradise they had sought throughout the United States and Europe.

In 1903, hot Santa Ana winds swept from the inland valleys toward the sea, and the most disastrous brush fire in Malibu's modern history destroyed the ornate Victorian-style mansion Rindge built at the base of Laudamus Hill. When Frederick Rindge died two years later at the age of forty-eight, May Rindge determined that she would protect the Malibu from the encroaching Los Angeles urban sprawl at any cost. To this

the first Rindge home, forced May to look for new income sources. One was the Malibu Potteries *(see the Malibu Lagoon State Beach–Adamson House entry)*; another was to sell portions of the beachfront for the Malibu Movie Colony *(see the Malibu Lagoon State Beach–Malibu Surfrider Beach entry)*. Due to

Tile-decorated doorway and patio, Adamson House, Malibu Lagoon State Beach

end, she spent the next thirty years locked in what ultimately were to be losing battles.

Beginning in 1907, May Rindge spent her fortune on a series of relentless conflicts in county, state, and federal courts. Her armed riders patrolled the ranch's fenced perimeter, turning back travelers, process servers, roadbuilders, and sheriff's deputies. It is rumored that some surveyors and engineers never returned from their encounters with May Rindge's riders, who periodically dynamited or plowed under new county roads. Mrs. Rindge's legal fees were astronomical. Ultimately, the half-million-dollar cost to build a mansion on Laudamus Hill in Malibu Canyon, above the site of

business complications, Mrs. Rindge's operating company was forced into bankruptcy in 1936, and in 1940 the entire Malibu ranch was put up for subdivision.

May Rindge, the "Queen of Malibu," died in 1941 at seventy-seven, nearly a pauper. Malibu is now an incorporated city that rivals the French and Italian rivieras, is home to the rich and famous and beach bum alike, is world famous as a recreational paradise, and yet retains much of the peace and natural beauty that gave Frederick Rindge so many "happy days in southern California." Today, we owe the relative serenity of these twenty-five miles of coast to the stubborn efforts of the "Queen of Malibu."

The movie industry has taken good advantage of this varied terrain. In 1941, the country club area was passed off as the country of Wales when the film *How Green Was My Valley* was made by Twentieth Century Fox. Later, it was a stand-in for Korea (*M★A★S★H*), Georgia (*Roots*), Utah (*Butch Cassidy and the Sundance Kid*), Kentucky (*Daniel Boone*), middle America (*Mr. Blandings Builds His Dream House*), tropical Africa (*Tarzan*), and even a future Earth (*Planet of the Apes*). Dozens of other movies and television shows have been filmed here by major studios, and even though the land was bought by the state for park purposes in 1975, traces of filmmaking activities remain, such as a military jeep and ambulance at the *M★A★S★H* filming site, a safe along High Road used for explosives, and fake bullet holes painted on the walls of the Mott Adobe.

To reach the park's visitor center, Hunter House, walk an easy .75 mile west on Crags Road from the day-use parking area. You'll pass the junction of Las Virgenes and Malibu creeks. Fishing is permitted with a California state fishing license.

The visitor center, with a slide show, book sales, and hands-on exhibits explaining local animals, plants, and Native American Indian history, is a great children's destination. From here, it's a short and easy walk on the spectacular **Gorge Trail** to the famous Rock Pool. Giant sycamores and exotic Deodar cedars on the way make good picnic sites. Malibu Creek flows into the pool via a boulder-choked passage through the gorge of Triunfo Canyon. (Portions of *Tarzan*, *South Pacific*, and the TV series *Swiss Family Robinson* were filmed here.) Swimming is allowed—there is no lifeguard

Tent camping, Malibu Creek State Park

Filmmaking continues in the park today.

Trails: The park boasts thirty-five miles of trails and fire roads. Bicycles are allowed only on fire roads; horses are permitted on all trails except where signed to the contrary.

service—but diving is strictly prohibited. Daring and agile climbers can press on through the water and over the boulders and cliff faces deep into the gorge and the Kaslow Natural Preserve, where golden eagles nest and mountain lions roam.

West of the visitor center, **Crags Road** climbs over a ridge to Century Reservoir, built in 1901 to provide water and recreational opportunities for the country club. The twenty-acre reservoir has partly silted in, forming a marsh where red-winged blackbirds nest and buffleheads, mallards, and coots may be seen. Ash and oak trees along the reservoir shade fine picnic spots. Swimming is allowed but not encouraged. Fishing for catfish, bass, and bluegill is allowed with a license; scuba divers inspecting the dam claim that monstrous bass lurk in these dark waters. West on Crags Road through wooded Triunfo Canyon, willows grow densely along the creek and belted kingfishers may be spotted diving for small fish. Fossil marine shells and fish occur in sedimentary rocks lining the gorge, and abalone-shell *middens* (trash heaps) in this area mark former Chumash encampments.

The beautiful .5-mile **Forest Trail**, running along the base of the hill on the south side of the reservoir, is an easy side trip through a grove of tall redwoods planted by members of the country club.

Crags Road eventually emerges into a valley on the south side of the Goat Buttes, where *M★A★S★H* (both the movie and television series) was filmed. When the set and surrounding canyons burned during the 1982 Agoura fire, Warner Brothers' producers simply worked the fire into the episode.

The rugged Udell Gorge Natural Preserve is just to the north. To the south, the Kaslow Natural Preserve stretches to the crest of the mountains and protects hidden waterfalls and relict populations of dogwood, big-leaf maple, and giant chain ferns in Fern and Mendenhall canyons.

The 1-mile **Yearling Trail** in the Reagan Ranch area along Mulholland Highway passes through a hanging valley perched above Triunfo Canyon and one of the finest wildflower meadows in the park; March through May are the best months for displays. The .5-mile **Deer Leg Trail** parallels this, but passes through a dense oak forest. At the east end of the valley the .3-mile **Cage Creek Trail** drops steeply down to Malibu Creek near Century Reservoir, and from a turnoff .2 miles east on Crags Road, the .9-mile **Lookout Trail** offers a scenic return loop up a grassy ridgeline studded with oaks.

In the north of the park, the Liberty Canyon Natural Preserve protects the southernmost stands of California valley oaks, in the deep, fertile flatland soils beside Las Virgenes Creek. Most of these largest of American oaks (up to a hundred feet in breadth) were burned for charcoal in earlier years or plowed under for urban development; the stands here are precious remnants of those once-great forests.

The .7-mile **Grasslands Trail** connects Crags Road with Mulholland Drive and the 3.2-mile **Talepop Trail**, which goes on to climb a grassy ridge and loops back via Las Virgenes Creek. Along the way, it passes the boarded-up Sepulveda Adobe and the White Oak Ranch. The California Department of Parks and Recreation is attempting to restore part of the grasslands at the ranch to their native condition.

Traveling up the 1.2-mile **Liberty Canyon Trail** you can briefly forget all about the twentieth century, so complete is the isolation from development. Live oaks and massive valley oaks mix together in the alternating chaparral, grassland, and thickets of coffeeberry, wild roses, and elderberry. But around the last bend to the north the pastoral scene has been plowed, and natural beauty

Goat Buttes, Malibu Creek State Park

first section, the Mesa Peak Fire Road, climbs eighteen hundred feet up a long ridge topped with cave-riddled sandstone boulders. Castro Peak Motorway brings you to Bulldog Road, where the Backbone Trail turns south, but you can complete the loop by turning north on Bulldog and making a dizzying 3.7-mile descent to Crags Road near the *M*A*S*H* set; follow Crags Road to the campground and Tapia Spur Trail.

Malibu Creek is the largest watershed in the Santa Monica Mountains, and the only one to extend completely through them, making it an important habitat linkage. No trails extend into its lower gorge below Tapia Park. Fishing restrictions apply on Malibu Creek and a license is required for persons sixteen and older. Fishing is closed from November 30 through the Saturday before Memorial Day and is prohibited below the dam.

Camping: The park's sixty-two-site campground (for use by tents or RVs up to eighteen feet) is in a beautiful, valley-oak-studded meadow that has excellent spring wildflower displays. Surrounding are low hills clothed in live oaks and chaparral. Camping specifics: fee for overnight stays; sites are available on first-come, first-served basis; restrooms, water, solar showers, picnic tables, charcoal stoves, sanitary dump station; no hookups are available. There is also a **group camp site** with similar facilities (but no dump station) that will accommodate up to fifty persons. For more information and to reserve, call MISTIX at (800) 444-PARK.

During dry periods, the park may be closed due to fire danger; call (805) 488-8147 for status.

replaced by the ubiquitous pink-tile roofs of tract-home suburbia, southern-California style.

Just west of the park's campground is the .4-mile wheelchair-accessible **Visually Impaired Trail**, signed in braille to interpret the oak forest, grasslands, and creekside habitat here. The .9-mile **Tapia Spur Trail** passes through the group camp for an easy walk through meadows and oak woodlands to Tapia Park and connections to the Backbone Trail.

The **Backbone Trail (east)** departs from the intersection of Malibu Canyon Road and Piuma Road; passes through a lush, riparian forest; and over a distance of 5.5 miles, steeply climbs fifteen hundred feet to Stunt Road. **The Backbone Trail (west)** affords a strenuous 14.5-mile loop through the high country and Triunfo Canyon. Starting at a small parking lot on Malibu Canyon Road just south of the Las Virgenes Water Treatment Plant, the trail's

21 Malibu Lagoon State Beach

Location: Pacific Coast Highway, Malibu; see map page vii

Administered by: California Department of Parks and Recreation (818) 880-0350

Hours: 8 A.M. to sunset

Fees: No entrance fee

Facilities: Chemical toilets, water, picnic tables

Parking: Paid parking in county lot west of Malibu Pier or state lot west of Malibu Creek

FYI: Take advantage of the trails, birdwatching tours in season, and interpretive panels. Alcohol, firearms, motor vehicles, bicycles, fires, camping, dogs, horses, swimming, rafts, and jet skis are prohibited.

A well-known surfing site; critical estuarine habitat for coastal species; and a rich human history, both prehistoric and modern, come together at Malibu Lagoon State Beach.

Malibu Lagoon is one of the few coastal lagoons remaining between Mugu Lagoon in Ventura County and Anaheim Bay in Orange County. Its brackish waters are a fertile nursery for many marine creatures, large and small. The lagoon is also an important rest and feeding area along the Pacific flyway, and over two hundred species of birds have been seen here. A California state fishing license is required for persons sixteen and older, and fishing is not allowed below the dam. Fishing is closed from November 30 through the Saturday before Memorial Day.

The Chumash built their largest and easternmost village on the shores of Malibu Lagoon. *Humaliwo* ("the surf sounds loudly") had a population of around a thousand, giving it one of the highest densities of any Native American Indian village north of Mexico. Here, the Chumash had easy launching for their *tomols* (plank boats) bound for fishing and trading expeditions along the coast and to the Channel Islands. Some historians believe Humaliwo may have been the Pueblo de las Canoas, the village where on October 10, 1542, the Spanish explorer Juan Cabrillo first encountered the Chumash people (others believe the site was at Point Mugu). At this village "there came to the ships many very good canoes, large enough for twelve or thirteen Indians." Archeological evidence shows that Humaliwo had been inhabited for twenty-five hundred years before the Spanish encounter and was perhaps at the peak of its development in 1542.

On the spit just to the east of Malibu Lagoon stands the stunningly beautiful **Adamson House**, designed in the Moorish and Spanish Mediterranean colonial-revival style by architect Stiles Clements. Completed in 1929, the forty-five-hundred-square-foot home was intended as a "beach house" for newly married Merritt Hutley Adamson and Rhoda Rindge, daughter of Frederick and May Rindge, the last owners of the Rancho Malibu Spanish land grant. Today, the house is the only building remaining from the Rindge empire.

The Adamson House is a veritable showcase of ceramic tile, an example of what could be done with the products of the Malibu Potteries. The potteries, started in 1926 by May Rindge, were located a half-mile to the east and took advantage of the buff and red clays mined from nearby hillsides. The state took over the house in 1968, and it was scheduled to be torn down to make way for a parking lot but was saved by the efforts of the Malibu Historical Society, which sponsors the Malibu Lagoon Museum in the converted garage. The house is now a California State Historical Landmark and is on the National Register of Historic Places. The grounds are open between 8 A.M. and sunset; Adamson House is open to the public on a guided-tour basis, 10 A.M. to 2 P.M., Wednesday through Saturday, group tours Tuesday by reservation. Call (310) 456-8432. The museum has exhibits depicting Malibu history and a gift shop.

The **Malibu Surfrider Beach** stretches for three-quarters of a mile along the point next to the Adamson House and Malibu Lagoon and is a series of rocky tidal flats most of the year. It is one of the few beaches anywhere devoted exclusively to surfing—swimming, rafts, and jet skis are prohibited. Malibu, with its rare point break, is the best surfing spot in southern California. Its southern swells, which roll onto this south-facing beach between May and October, peel off the point in regular, predictable sets. Waves run up to twelve feet high and give fast takeoffs and rides of up to a quarter-mile on well-shaped curls. Up to two hundred surfers may be in the waters off the point (which average sixty-three degrees F.) at any one time. To help keep traffic orderly, surfers have a tacit agreement that in busy times, First Point (the westernmost set of breaks) is reserved for boards less than eight feet long; Third Point (closest to Malibu Pier) is reserved for boards eight feet or longer. Third Point is considered to give some of the best long-board waves in the world. The first great surfer at Malibu was

Hawaiian Duke Kahanamoku, who helped introduce surfing to California in 1927, using boards up to eighteen feet long and weighing over one hundred pounds.

A lifeguard is on duty year-round, and surfing is allowed all day, every day of the year.

The Malibu Movie Colony, on the beach just west of the point, was the first major suburban development on the Malibu coast, leased and/or sold by cash-poor May Rindge beginning in 1928 to motion-picture greats of the time: Jackie Coogan, Dolores del Rio, Gary Cooper, Clara Bow, Barbara Stanwyck, and Bing Crosby. The Colony remains one of the most exclusive residential communities of the famous and influential.

22 Malibu Pier

Location: Pacific Coast Highway, Malibu; see map page vii

Administered by: California Department of Parks and Recreation (818) 880-0350

Hours: Sunrise to sunset; pier locked at 6 P.M.

Fees: No entrance fee

Facilities: Restroom, water, restaurant, bait-and-tackle shop, commercial sport fishing boats

Parking: Limited free street parking; paid parking lot to east, and county lot at Malibu Lagoon State Beach to west

FYI: The Malibu Coast Fault, this area's most significant geologic factor, passes underwater and comes ashore nearby.

Historic seven-hundred-foot-long Malibu Pier, in the

cove called Keller's shelter after an early owner of the Malibu coast, offers views of the central Santa Monica Bay and is a comfortable place to watch world-class surfers on the point break at adjacent Malibu Surfrider Beach. Benches surrounding the pier's bait-and-tackle shop are quiet places to while away an afternoon fishing for halibut, mackerel, bass, and perch. The pier is the only place in the national recreation area that you can board a commercial sport-fishing boat for a half-day trip.

Lobster

23 Nicholas Canyon County Beach

Location: Pacific Coast Highway, Malibu; see map page v

Administered by: Los Angeles County Beaches and Harbors
(310) 305-9503

Hours: Sunrise to sunset

Fees: No entrance fee

Facilities: Restrooms, water, picnic tables

Parking: Paid parking

FYI: Alcohol, firearms, motor vehicles, bicycles, fires, camping, dogs, horses, boat launching, inflatable flotation devices, and jet skis are prohibited.

Once the site of beachside homes, including that of actor Vincent Price, Nicholas Canyon County Beach (sometimes known as Point Zero) is today a destination for surfing, scuba diving, and picnicking. Its mellow atmosphere and seclusion

from the noise and bustle of the Pacific Coast Highway make it an attractive spot.

Kelp beds and small reefs are close in, populated by abalone, lobsters, and sea urchins. The clean water indicated by these sea creatures' presence makes for good scuba diving. It is less than optimal for swimming, but the rocky point break at the eastern end of the beach is a popular surfing site. The surf at this sandy beach tends to break close to the shore because of the beach's steep angle.

Those who don't want to get wet can view the ocean and surfing action from the bluffs above, or stroll westward as far as Sequit Point at Leo Carrillo State Beach, about a mile distant. Nicholas Canyon, unlike most beaches in the Los Angeles area, still has remnants of the plant community known as coastal strand. This transitional community runs from the beach to the bluffs and is composed of drought-hearty and salt-tolerant plants such as sand verbena, beach morning glory, and sea rocket. Also watch for small animals here—kingsnakes, gopher snakes, rabbits, and skunks abound.

24 Palisades Park

Location: Ocean Avenue, Santa Monica; see map page viii

Administered by: City of Santa Monica, Community and Cultural Services, Parks and Sports Division (310) 393-7593, Visitor Information Booth

Hours: 5 A.M. to midnight

Fees: No entrance fee

Facilities: Restroom, water, picnic tables

Parking: Metered curbside parking on Ocean Avenue, limited street parking on Pacific Coast Highway

FYI: Alcohol, firearms, motor vehicles, bicycles, skateboards, fires, camping, dogs, and horses are prohibited.

Once the western terminus of Route 66, the famous transcontinental vagabond highway, Palisades Park stretches for almost two miles along Santa Monica's Ocean Avenue above Santa Monica State Beach.

Spacious lawns shaded by more than a thousand trees beckon on hot summer days. Mexican fan palms, Canary Island date palms, towering eucalyptus, and more than thirty other species of semi-tropical trees were planted here beginning in 1908. Gardens of succulents and shrubs, both exotic and native, dot the grounds and cascade down sandstone bluffs. These bluffs, ranging from 40 to 125 feet high, were formed from materials washed down from the mountains as long as 3 million years ago.

More than twenty thousand visitors come here on an average weekend to amble or jog the length of the park along level, paved walkways or to rest on the many benches and enjoy panoramic views of the sun sinking over Santa Monica Bay. Stairs provide access to the beaches via overpasses across the Pacific Coast Highway. A recreation center for seniors is a popular gathering place for cultural and social activities. Children will especially enjoy the Camera Obscura, a periscopic fisheye lens that allows visitors to "spy" on beachgoers. Other

The Mulholland Scenic Corridor

Like Malibu and Bel Air, Mulholland Drive is a name of almost-legendary proportions, part of the southern California mystique. It is famed as a lovers' lane, an illicit dragstrip, and as the place to look down on the twinkling lights of all Los Angeles.

Within the Los Angeles city limits, the route is called Mulholland Drive; outside, it is Mulholland Highway. All of it is within the national recreation area. Conceived in 1913 by Los Angeles City Engineer William Mulholland, with construction beginning in 1924, it was intended as a low-speed scenic recreational corridor that would give access to mountain parks and link the city with the sea. It does just that, stretching from Hollywood at Cahuenga Pass to the Pacific at Sequit Point in Leo Carrillo State Beach, just short of the Ventura county line. It is the only road to run lengthwise through most of the Santa Monica Mountains, and for much of its fifty-five miles, it travels close to the mountain crest, which gives magnificent views of the city in its eastern half, and of mountain wilds in its western half.

attractions include an Alaskan totem pole at the north end of the park, two 1861-vintage cannons near the southern end, a monument to the discovery of Santa Monica Bay by Juan Cabrillo in 1542, and a statue of Santa Monica, the saint for whom the city was named.

Volunteers at the visitor information kiosk on Ocean Avenue near Arizona Street can answer questions about activities and facilities in the Santa Monica area.

25 Paramount Ranch

Location: Cornell Road, Agoura Hills; see map page vi

Administered by: National Park Service (818) 597-9192, ext. 201 for information or
(818) 597-1036, ext. 223 for permits and reservations

Hours: Open twenty-four hours

Fees: No entrance fee

Facilities: Restrooms, water, picnic tables, telephone. Weddings, group activities for fifty or more, catered food, and paid entertainment must have permits. Pavilion with stage, electricity, tables available for group use by permit.

Parking: Free NPS lot open 8 A.M. to sunset

FYI: Firearms, motor vehicles, fires, and camping are prohibited. Dogs must be on leash.

Historic Paramount Ranch offers opportunities for picnicking and nature study and is a favorite place for cultural events, weddings, or other large group gatherings. But it's most famous for its long history as a motion-picture filming site and for its Western Town set, where even today you stand a good chance of encountering filmmaking crews almost any day of the week.

Most recently, the television series *Dr. Quinn, Medicine Woman* was filmed here. The Western Town set represents Colorado Springs as it is seen in the television series. As other film companies come into Paramount Ranch, Western Town will be modified to meet their needs. The building now called Bray's Mercantile has been a saloon, a Conoco gas station, and a Spanish mission. Walking through Western Town can bring a myriad of surprises. Close inspection reveals that rock walls are fiberglass and old buildings are in reality quite new.

You're welcome to wander the streets of Western Town and watch filming crews at work; please respect the needs of crews to close certain areas and have silence at critical times. Park rangers regularly give guided walks here.

Main Street in Western Town boasts a motley assemblage of stereotypically western buildings, some nothing more than false fronts with windows that open into nowhere. The saloon has low eaves on the porch to make men

standing there look taller, while the hotel opposite has extra-tall eaves to make women standing under them look shorter. This is the stuff of illusion.

By 1921, Jesse Laskey, co-owner and producer for Paramount Studios (then known as Famous Players-Laskey-Paramount Pictures), had made so many western films at Paramount's ranch in Burbank that movie-goers were beginning to recognize the sets and terrain from one movie to the next. In search of a remedy, he leased and later bought four thousand acres near Agoura, part of the old Spanish land grant Rancho Las Virgenes. Within this relatively small area, Laskey found the variety of terrain so necessary to his trade, the marketing of illusions: brush-covered slopes, boulders, rugged Sugarloaf Mountain, oak forests, creekside thickets, and rolling grasslands. For the next twenty-five years, Paramount filmed here, with backdrop of a giant fortress for the production of *The Adventures of Marco Polo*, ostensibly set in China.

In 1946, the just-ended war, the beginnings of television, and a judgment forcing Paramount to sell its chain of theaters caused the studio to fall on hard times, and they sold the ranch. In 1952, William Hertz bought the 326 acres that make up the current Paramount Ranch. In addition to renting the ranch for recreational events such as equestrian shows, square dances, barbecues,

Main Street, Western Town set, Paramount Ranch

as many as five hundred people per day working out of on-site warehouses that housed props, a woodworking studio, a commissary, a bunkhouse, a small "tent city," ranch house, barns and corrals, plus sets brought from the Burbank site. The many films made here include *The Scarlet Letter* (1926), *The Man from Wyoming* (1930), *The Maid of Salem* (1937), and *Under the Light of the Western Stars* (1925). In 1937 the ranch "became" San Francisco for *Wells Fargo*, and a horde of elephants and two thousand decorated horses were gathered against a

pow wows, and dog trials, Hertz allowed independent film production companies to continue the tradition of filmmaking. The National Park Service revitalized the sets in 1984. The ranch was busy with crews filming most of the westerns shown on television in the mid-fifties, such as *The Cisco Kid*, *Bat Masterson*, and *The Plunderers*.

Under a string of new owners, various recreational, sporting, and filming activities continued at the ranch. In 1980, when owners planned to subdivide the land and build 159 homes, the National Park Service bought the ranch for $6 million. The National Park Service is continuing with traditional uses, including filming and large public events, and adding the new element of environmental and historical interpretation. Guided walks through Western Town are regularly given; see *Outdoors*, the National Park Service's schedule of activities, for times. A large pavilion with a stage is the scene of an annual historical film festival, "Silents Under the Stars," and may be rented for weddings, company picnics, or other group activities. The grounds are host to the Topanga Banjo and Fiddle Contest and the Pumpkin Festival.

The **Coyote Canyon Nature Trail** is an easy .75-mile round-trip walk or ride on which you can see chamise, scrub oak, elderberry, and other chaparral plants and get a closer look at Sugarloaf Mountain. You'll also find a nice picnic site and a good view of the valley. The **5K Run Trail** is a 3.1-mile loop run criss-crossing the wide variety of terrain that attracted Paramount Studios to this site. The ranch is also a popular take-off site for hikes through the Reagan Ranch area of adjacent Malibu Creek State Park.

Paramount Ranch is near the southernmost limit of the valley oak's distribution. Most young oaks here have been destroyed by grazing, farming, recreational and filmmaking activities, and building. The National Park Service is experimenting with oak regeneration techniques such as planting, restricting trampling, prescribed fires, and encouragement of native grasses.

26 Peter Strauss Ranch

Location: Mulholland Highway, Agoura Hills; see map page vi

Administered by: National Park Service (818) 597-9192, ext. 201

Hours: Open twenty-four hours. House and art gallery opened only for special events.

Fees: No entrance fee

Facilities: Restrooms, water, picnic tables, playground

Parking: Free NPS lot; open 8 A.M. to 5 P.M. daily

FYI: Dogs must be on leash. Firearms, motor vehicles, bicycles, fires, and camping are prohibited.

Amid the lush eucalyptus groves and oak- and sycamore-bowered grounds of Peter Strauss Ranch there is evidence that this site has long been a retreat and recreational fantasyland in the best southern California tradition. The white-banistered stone ranch house and tiny stone caretaker's cottage along with a giant outdoor aviary remind us of how Harry Miller, an automotive engineer who invented the carburetor, developed the ranch in 1923 and stocked it with wild or exotic animals such as parrots, monkeys, and bears. In the early 1930s, two Malibou Lake entrepreneurs, Warren Shobert and Arthur Edeson, began to develop the site as "Shoson," a children's fantasyland, and left us the white entrance arch to the parking area that is the ranch's trademark today.

Sections of the dam built in the 1940s across adjacent Triunfo Creek can be seen. Lake Enchanto, formed by the dam, was a popular site for fishing, swimming, and boating until the dam washed out in a 1969 flood.

When the ranch was owned by Charles Hinman, the "Enchanto experience" was in vogue, especially in the 1950s, when crowds came from the city for the amusement rides, summer camps, and parties.

An important part of this experience was a swim in the 140-foot-diameter circular pool, which remains but is no longer used; it could accommodate up to three thousand people and was among the largest pools in the West at the time. In its center was an island from which people dived and bands played while audiences lounged on hillside terraces shaded by live oaks (one of which is significant as a corner for the Rancho Las Virgenes Spanish land grant). The house's patio of imported Italian marble terrazzo was the scene of "Big Band" concerts and dances in the 1940s, and in the 1950s, of concerts by country-western singers such as Johnny Cash and Willie Nelson. Emmy Award-winning actor and producer Peter Strauss bought the ranch in 1977, rebuilt the home and planted the cactus gardens and lawns, and in 1983 sold it for use as a public park.

Today, Peter Strauss Ranch is among the most popular locations in the Santa Monica Mountains for outdoor weddings. Spacious, tree-shaded creekside lawns are perfect for ceremonies, and the terrazzo patio invites dancing. The house is now used as a conference room and art gallery, open only on special occasions. A variety of art shows is also held on the grounds, with the Golden State Sculpture Association show a long-standing favorite. A hillside amphitheater is the site of a series of free summer concerts by a diverse collection of musical groups, ranging from popular to New Age, Irish, and African.

Triunfo Creek offers creekside viewing of riparian and aquatic plants and animals. The .6-mile **Peter Strauss Trail** is an easy trip for the novice hiker as it traverses the steep hillside above the ranch house; live oaks, scrub oaks, and California bay trees may be seen on the way. Beware of poison oak and ticks.

Call (818) 597-9192 ext. 223 to reserve dates for weddings or special events, or ext. 201 for information on the summer concert series.

27 Point Dume State Beach

Location: Westward Beach Road, Malibu; see map page vi

Administered by: California Department of Parks and Recreation (818) 880-0350

Hours: 8 A.M. to sunset

Fees: No entrance fee

Facilities: No facilities provided

Parking: Free street parking on Westward Beach Road; limited free street parking on Dume Drive (observe signed parking restrictions); fee parking in L.A. County parking lot

FYI: Alcohol, firearms, motor vehicles, bicycles, glass containers, fires, camping, dogs, and horses are prohibited.

Rocky cliffs studded with caves, secluded beaches, outlying reefs and kelp beds, and sandy hillsides combine to make Point Dume one of the outstanding natural beachside areas remaining along the L.A. County coast. The point's two-hundred-fifty-foot elevation and strategic prominence at the western end of Santa Monica Bay also make this the best place south of Santa Barbara to see migrating whales.

The California gray whale is most commonly seen; these fifty-foot-long mammals generally pass southward in December and January, en route from the Bering Sea to mating grounds in Baja California, and can sometimes be seen heading north in March. You'll also notice that the wave-battered rocks off the point are white with the guano of roosting cormorants and pelicans.

California poppy

At the summit of Point Dume, you will find an area leveled by U.S. Marines in World War II, and a sign commemorating the naming of the point in 1793 by the English explorer George Vancouver for his friend, Father Francisco Dumetz of Mission San Buenaventura. The point was then, and remains, an important navigational landmark.

On a clear day, you can see a thirty-mile sweep of coastline east to the Palos Verdes Peninsula. Beautiful Dume Cove lies at the foot of the point to the east; a trail down the bluffs meets the beach, which, at low tide, can be walked to Paradise Cove. To the west are Westward Beach and Zuma Beach, two and one-half miles of sandy shore. Visible below is Pirate's Cove, for decades a smugglers' landing and until recent years famed as a "clothing-optional" beach. This area offers excel-

lent picnicking, sunbathing, and tidepool exploring.

Drying, salt-laden winds off the ocean make the point a desert, and the seabluff's coastal strand community of drought-adapted plants is well developed. You'll find bladder pod, canyon sunflower, and California poppy as well as two native cliffside succulents that reach their southern limits here: giant coreopsis and live-forever.

28 Point Mugu Naval Air Weapons Station/Mugu Lagoon

Location: Pacific Coast Highway, Point Mugu; see map page iv

Administered by: United States Navy (805) 989-1110

Hours: Prearranged organization tours only

Fees: No entrance fee

Facilities: None

Parking: Roadside pullouts on Pacific Coast Highway

FYI: Cameras and video equipment are prohibited. Visitors to the naval station must obey all U.S. Navy rules and regulations.

Beginning one-half mile northwest of Point Mugu is Mugu Lagoon, the largest coastal wetland in southern California. At the mouth of

Canada geese

Calleguas Creek, the lagoon is entirely within the boundaries of the United States Naval Air Weapons Station. You can view the lagoon and its abundant animal life from roadside pullouts on the Pacific Coast Highway, or by accompanying periodic prearranged organization tours offered by the U.S. Navy.

Wetlands such as Mugu Lagoon are the richest and biologically most productive of all marine environments. They act as food factories and sheltered breeding grounds for animals at all levels in the food chain, which then enrich the adjacent, less-fertile ocean.

Mugu Lagoon is famous for its bird life. While the largest flocks of migratory birds tend to pass by offshore, pintails, brant, and Canada geese are frequently seen, along with common loons. Shore birds by the thousands frequent the sand spits, and raptors such as hawks, kites, kestrels, and owls prowl the salt grass and pickleweed flats. Six birds officially listed as threatened or endangered are found here: the California brown pelican, light-footed clapper rail, California least tern, peregrine falcon, western snowy plover, and Belding's savanna sparrow.

The large Chumash village of Muwu, from which the name Mugu was derived, was located near the mouth of the lagoon in an area that had been inhabited for several thousand years. Here, the Chumash found an abundance of fish, shellfish, birds, and plants for food. Point Mugu was also an easily recognizable landmark for Chumash paddling their plank boats on trading expeditions from the Channel Islands.

29 Point Mugu State Park

Location: West Pacific Coast Highway, Malibu; see map page iv

Administered by: California Department of Parks and Recreation (805) 986-8591

Hours: Open twenty-four hours

Fees: No entrance fee; fee for overnight camping; fee for parking lot at Big Sycamore Canyon (no fee for hikers or mountain bikers)

Facilities: Restrooms, water, picnic tables, backcountry camping (individual/group/equestrian)

Parking: Paid parking

FYI: Backcountry areas may be evacuated and closed to entry during periods of high fire danger. Bicycles are restricted to fire roads and designated trails and motor vehicles are restricted to frontcountry campgrounds. No dogs in the backcountry and must be on leash elsewhere. See camp entries for further specifics. Alcohol and firearms are prohibited.

Of all the parklands in the region, Point Mugu State Park is the largest, wildest, and most remote from metropolitan areas. At the westernmost tip of the Santa Monica Mountains, the park embraces five miles of rocky shoreline tempered with broad, sandy beaches; a relict tall-grass prairie; a major canyon system and the finest sycamore savanna in southern California; and the vast chaparral-cloaked heartland of the Boney Mountain State Wilderness. The park's high point, three-thousand-foot Tri-Peaks, receives snow most years though it is less than five miles from the ocean. The beaches of Point Mugu offer the most extensive picnic and camping facilities on this coastline, and are filled every day from mid-June through September. In the backcountry (a state-designated wilderness), opportunities for solitude are unsurpassed, and the park's seventy-five miles of trails and fire roads offer outstanding hiking, horseback and bike riding. Backcountry areas may be evacuated and closed during periods of high fire danger; call (805) 488-8147 for status.

Ancestors of the Chumash lived here for at least six thousand years, prospering in the area's abundance. Within sixty years after establishment of the nearby Mission San Buenaventura by Father Junipero Serra in 1783 and the development of El Camino Real to the north, most of the Chumash had succumbed to European diseases or been forced (or enticed) to leave their land and enter service at the mission or area ranchos. Only a few holdouts remained in the Mugu hills, maintaining what they could of their traditional lifeways.

northern part of the present park and the adjacent Rancho Sierra Vista, among other lands. In 1836, the thirty-thousand-acre Rancho Guadalasca was granted by the Mexican territorial governor to Isabel Maria Yorba, who raised cattle on this isolated spread until 1851, when she sold twenty-two thousand acres to a land company.

In 1873, William R. Broome of Santa Barbara bought the land; part of it remains in the Broome family today as an active cattle ranch and farm. In 1966, the state bought a portion of Rancho Guadalasca from the Broomes, forming what is now the southern part of the park, and in 1972, the Danielson family sold Sycamore Canyon and the western slope of Boney Mountain to the state at half their market price, completing the present park holdings.

The name "Mugu" is derived from the Chumash word *muwu*, roughly translated as "beach." Point Mugu may have been where, in October 1542, Spanish explorer Juan Cabrillo and his men dropped anchor and may have first encountered the Chumash, who paddled out in their *tomols*, or plank boats.

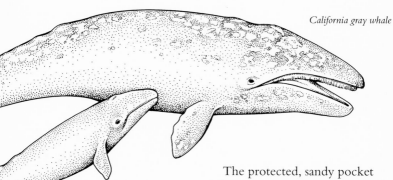

California gray whale

In 1803, the partitioning of Chumash lands at Point Mugu began when a grazing and use permit was granted to former Spanish soldier José Ignacio Rodriguez for Rancho El Conejo, which included the

The protected, sandy pocket beach at **Sycamore Cove**, bounded on both sides by rocky headlands, is a good site for sunbathing, fishing, and beachside picnicking under shade trees. California gray whales are sometimes sighted during the spring. Sycamore Cove is a fee area for day use only, between the hours of 8 A.M. and sunset. You will find seasonal lifeguard service, a picnic area with fifty tables and stoves, chemical toilets, water, a wheelchair ramp to the beach, and an off-street parking lot.

To the northwest is **Thornhill Broome Memorial Beach Campground**, where the wide beach varies from cobbled to sandy and offers good surf fishing and beachcombing. While lifeguard service is provided in season, swimming here is best reserved for the hardy and experienced; all the waters on this part of the coast are cold and rough, but especially so in the vicinity of Point Mugu due to westerly exposures and cold water flowing up from an underwater canyon just off the point. For thousands of years, prevailing westerly winds have swept along this stretch of beach and piled sand high on the slope of the jutting headland at the mouth of Big Sycamore Canyon, resulting in the Great Sand Dune.

There are eighty sites for tents and RVs up to thirty feet, but no hookups. There is a limit of two vehicles and eight persons per site, and chemical toilets, water, picnic tables, and charcoal stoves are available. Year-round camping reservations may be made through MISTIX, (800) 444-PARK.

Big Sycamore Canyon is a parking fee area for day use only between the hours of 8 A.M. and sunset. Picnicking is allowed at the Danielson and Sycamore multiuse areas, where restrooms, water, picnic tables, and charcoal stoves are provided. One of the premier hiking, bike, and horseback riding experiences in the recreation area is the mountains-to-the-sea trip

down the 8-mile **Big Sycamore Canyon Trail**, which begins in the north in the grasslands of Rancho Sierra Vista and drops down a steep grade on a narrow, paved road. The rest of the trail is level and easy, with 3.5 miles of pavement and then dirt track.

At **Sycamore Canyon Campground**, there are fifty-five sites for tents or RVs up to thirty feet, and two handicap sites; restrooms, water, solar showers, picnic tables, charcoal stoves, and a dump station are provided. There is a limit of two vehicles and six people per campsite. There is also one hiker/mountain biker site, which can accommodate up to ten campers. Sites are available by reservation through MISTIX, (800) 444-PARK.

From Sycamore Canyon Campground, you can explore Big Sycamore Canyon, with its intermittent stream and abundant wildlife; climb the surrounding chaparral-cloaked ridges, reached by the nearby **Scenic Trail** and **Overlook Trail**; or lounge on the beach at adjacent Sycamore Cove or near Thornhill Broome Memorial Beach Campground. Rangers lead nature walks from here, and give evening campfire talks at the amphitheater. There are no

Monarch butterflies

Boney Ridge, Point Mugu State Park

hookups but there are restrooms, water, solar showers, picnic tables, charcoal stoves, and a dump station. Sites are available by reservations through MISTIX, (800) 444-PARK.

Beginning in October in some years, masses of orange-and-black monarch butterflies arrive to spend the winter, settling in the eucalyptus trees near the campground and escaping the freezing temperatures of Canada and the northern U.S. This sheltered grove, with its dappled sunlight and abundant nectar-bearing shrubs, is an ideal roost for these migrating insects. Look, but please do not collect or disturb—like all plants, animals, and other features in the national and state parks, butterflies are protected.

The Danielson Multiuse Area, along the **Backbone Trail** and **Big Sycamore Canyon Trail**, has a group camping area for mountain-bikers, hikers, or horse groups; vehicle-access group use is also allowed. A fireplace, barbecue pit with rock patio, and solar showers are special amenities of Danielson. This is one of the area's three group camps, and can accommodate groups of ten to fifty people and twenty-five horses. Restrooms, water, charcoal stoves, and a horse

trough are available. Advance reservations (two to six weeks ahead of time) are necessary; call (805) 488-5223. Vehicle access is via a steep, narrow road through the north park entrance, with ranger escort; all group members and vehicles must arrive and leave at the same time. Amplified music is prohibited.

The nearby **Sycamore Multiuse Area** is also reserved for groups of ten to twenty-five people. Among the amenities are chemical toilets, water, a fire ring, barbecue, horse trough, and pipe corrals. Available by reservation only, two to six weeks in advance; call (805) 488-5223. As with the Danielson area, vehicle access is via a steep, narrow road through the north park entrance, with ranger escort; all group members and vehicles must arrive and leave at the same time; and amplified music is prohibited.

Big Sycamore Canyon is the heart of the state park. The headwaters rise on the north slope of Tri-Peaks, and can be reached by the **Old Boney Trail** from the park's northern Potrero Valley entrance through Rancho Sierra Vista.

Most of the area east of Big Sycamore Canyon is included in the six-thousand-acre Boney

Mountain State Wilderness. Motor vehicles, bicycles, and mechanized equipment are prohibited and no overnight camping is allowed. The eight-mile **Old Boney Road** cuts off the **Old Boney Trail** in the north end of the park and wanders south through deep canyons harboring hidden seeps and over steep chaparral ridges, spiked with stalks of white yucca flowers in late spring. The massive volcanic cliffs of Boney Mountain loom above, though they may be obscured by low winter clouds. This is home to mountain lions, golden eagles, and endangered peregrine falcons, and is sacred to the Chumash of the area.

Side trails include a **trail to Tri-Peaks**, the highest point on the mountain; a portion of the uncompleted **Backbone Trail** and the **Blue Canyon Trail**, which connect with the Big Sycamore Canyon Trail at the Danielson Multiuse Area; and the **Serrano Canyon Trail**, which leads through the narrow, one-thousand-foot-deep rock gorge of Serrano Canyon and emerges into Serrano Valley, a supremely peaceful, seldom-visited grassland surrounded by high cliffs. You can walk west about two miles through the valley to an alternate trailhead at the end of Serrano Road, off Cotherin and Yerba Buena roads.

Numerous trails wind through the hills and valleys to the west of Big Sycamore Canyon, offshoots of the Big Sycamore Canyon Trail. Paved **Ranch Center Road** is an easy ride or walk through grasslands, with excellent spring displays of clarkia, shooting stars, and other wildflowers. The trail connects upper Big Sycamore

Yucca

Canyon with the Ranch Center at the base of the westernmost range of mountains in the park; the Broome Ranch (Rancho Guadalasca) is just beyond. The **Hidden Pond Trail**, which can be used by hikers and equestrians but not mountain bikers, parallels Ranch Center Road most of the way by detouring steeply up to a ridgeline for good views of Big Sycamore Canyon and Boney Mountain. The "hidden pond" has water only in wet years.

Just before Ranch Center, the **Coyote Trail** heads south all the way down a ridgeline to Big Sycamore Canyon. From Ranch Center itself, the **Wood Canyon Trail** gently descends through a dense canopy of oaks down narrow Wood Canyon to Deer Camp Junction, where you'll find picnic tables, a toilet, and water. From just before the junction, the **Guadalasca Trail** branches northwest up a wooded canyon and climbs steadily to the highest ridgeline.

From Deer Camp Junction, the **Overlook Trail** heads southwest up a steep, rocky fire road that mountain-bikers call "Hell Hill" to the edge of La Jolla Valley. The trail then turns south to follow the high ridgeline between Big Sycamore Canyon and La Jolla Valley, with outstanding views on both sides as well as across to Boney Ridge and to the Channel Islands and the Pacific. From here, the trail descends steeply to Big Sycamore Canyon. Along the way is a junction with the **Scenic Trail**, a combination that makes a nice two-mile loop from Sycamore Canyon Campground.

About 1.5 miles up the Overlook Trail from Big Sycamore Canyon, the **Backbone Trail** branches south and drops steeply to the Ray Miller Trailhead in La Jolla Canyon, at the Pacific Coast Highway. This is the western terminus of the uncompleted Backbone Trail. The Ray Miller Trailhead at the base of the canyon serves two trails and offers a group campground. The Ray Miller Trail climbs from here to the Overlook Trail on the high ridge above. At the **Ray Miller Trailhead Group Camp**, there is space for one group of fifty people; facilities include restrooms, water, solar showers, picnic tables, and fire rings. Space is available by reservation through MISTIX, (800) 444-PARK.

The **La Jolla Canyon Trail** is the takeoff point for adventures in La Jolla Valley, one and one-half miles inland, and the backpack campsites there. Birders should note that the canyon is the home of the endangered least Bell's vireo. The **La Jolla Valley Walk-in Camp** is one of only two backpacking campsites in the national recreation area; its semi-primitive sites are set in a grove of small oaks. The sites are allocated on a first-come, first-served basis; self register and pay the fee at the trailhead. Available only by a two-mile hike from Ray Miller Trailhead on Pacific Coast Highway, or a five-mile hike from Sycamore Canyon Campground; no bicycles are allowed. There are nine sites, with a maximum of eight people per site. There is also one group camp for up to twenty-five people. Facilities include a horse corral, water, chemical toilets, and picnic tables. No open fires are allowed but camp stoves are permitted.

La Jolla Valley, tucked away in the park's far western corner, is an isolated world unto itself. It is an oak-studded, rolling grassland surrounded by an arc of high ridges dominated by Laguna Peak (with its surrealistic navy radar facility),

La Jolla Peak, and Mugu Peak. The area is designated as the La Jolla Valley Natural Preserve and is recognized as one of the finest of the few remnants of perennial bunchgrass prairies that formerly covered perhaps a quarter of the state of California. Most such prairies have been paved over, plowed under, or so heavily grazed that exotic weedy grasses have replaced the native species. In La Jolla Valley, such disturbances have been limited and several solid stands of purple needlegrass remain in the shallow rocky soil, especially near the edges of the valley. To protect this environment, bicycles and motor vehicles are prohibited. Most hikers enter via the La Jolla Canyon Trail from the Ray Miller Trailhead on Pacific Coast Highway, but it can also be reached by way of the seemingly vertical **Chumash Trail** from the Pacific Coast Highway or by the longer **Overlook Trail** from Deer Camp Junction. The Chumash Trail departs from the Pacific Coast Highway two miles west of the Ray Miller Trailhead, ascends steeply through giant coreopsis and prickly pear cactus, then drops into La Jolla Valley. Crushed shells litter the path, evidence of the popularity of this route with the Chumash. The **Mugu Peak Trail** turns off the trail at the ridgeline and affords scenic views from nine hundred feet above the ocean.

The easy **La Jolla Valley Loop Trail** circles around the broadest part of the valley and upper La Jolla Canyon. There are many archeological sites throughout this area, as this was an important gathering site for the Chumash. These people harvested native grass seeds, wild bulbs, and acorns, and hunted deer, rabbits, birds, and other game. A small pond in the northeast corner of the valley is a good place to look for resting migratory waterfowl, resident coots, and nesting red-winged blackbirds. Oaks here make a good picnic site, and the La Jolla Valley Walk-in Camp is nearby.

A series of small beaches with turbulent water lie to either side of rugged Point Mugu itself. There is seasonal lifeguard service at Mugu Beach; other beaches have limited free parking on Pacific Coast Highway but no facilities. The rocks around the point offer good fishing for rockfish and view-sites for the seals and sea lions that occasionally visit the point. Beware of sneaker waves; many drownings of inattentive anglers have occurred here.

30 Rancho Sierra Vista/Satwiwa

Location: Potrero Road, Newbury Park; see map page v

Administered by: National Park Service (818) 597-9192, ext. 201

Hours: Open twenty-four hours

Fees: No entrance fee

Facilities: Restrooms, water, picnic tables

Parking: Free NPS lot; open 8 A.M. to sunset

FYI: Bicycles are allowed only on the Wendy, Pinehill, and Rancho Overlook trails, and the trail to Big Sycamore Canyon. Horses permitted on all trails except in Satwiwa Native American Indian Natural Area. Firearms, motor vehicles, fires, and camping are prohibited.

The old West meets the new at Rancho Sierra Vista/Satwiwa, nestled beneath the dramatic ramparts of Boney Mountain at the edge of suburban Newbury Park. The park is

devoted to the preservation and interpretation of two cultural legacies—Native American Indian (especially the indigenous Chumash and Tongva/Gabrieliño) and the equestrian tradition of the early Spanish and later American ranchers. The image of the Spanish vaquero mounted on a noble steed and riding across rolling, oak-studded grasslands is one of the most dramatic symbols of old California. Here you will find hints of history, encounters with modern Native American Indians, and entrance into the vast interior backcountry of the Santa Monica Mountains.

Satwiwa Native American Indian Natural Area: Long before this land was ranched by Europeans, it was a thoroughfare, gathering ground, and village site for the Chumash. The Chumash were among the wealthiest and most sophisticated tribes in North America, living well on the abundance of wild foods and useful materials in their diverse homeland, which stretched from the ocean to the heights of the mountains and depths of the inland valleys. Today, the Rancho Sierra Vista area is called "Satwiwa," after a prehistoric Chumash village site nearby. *Satwiwa* means "the bluffs," and is thought to refer to the massive cliffs of Boney Mountain looming just to the south.

Satwiwa was on one of the main Chumash trade trails, running from the ocean to the inland valleys through Big Sycamore Canyon. Here, the Chumash gathered wild grass seed, brodiaea bulbs, and acorns from grasslands and oak savanna; *chia* (sage) seed and wild cherry pits from hillside chaparral; and hides from the abundant deer and rabbits. They traded these items for fish, otter pelts, abalone shell, asphaltum, soapstone bowls, and shell-bead money from the coast, and pine nuts and pine pitch from the mountain Chumash farther inland. Their trade trail extended hundreds of miles inland to the Mojave and Yokuts peoples along the Colorado River and in the San Joaquin Valley, who offered obsidian for arrowheads and knives, parrot feathers from Mexico, the red mineral pigment hematite, woven cotton blankets, tobacco, and sugar cakes of aphid honeydew.

No trace of the original Satwiwa can be seen today by the casual visitor, but in its place a new Satwiwa is rising in the form of the **Native American Indian Culture Center**. The center is a gathering ground for modern Chumash, Tongva/ Gabrieliño, and Native American Indians of other tribes; they come here to practice their traditional ceremonials. It is esti- mated that more Native American Indians live in the Los Angeles metropolitan area than on any reserva- tion in the country, and weekly events at Satwiwa provide you with an opportunity to meet Native American Indian ambassadors in person and learn about their cultures. Every Sunday, Native American Indian guest-hosts lead walks, perform ceremonies, or give talks or demonstrations on native crafts such as stone carving, basket weaving, or the preparation of native foods. All events are free and open to the general public.

The center is a cooperative venture between the National Park Service, the UCLA Graduate School of Architecture and Urban Planning, and the Friends of Satwiwa. When completed, it will include an outdoor amphitheater in a traditional "gathering ring" circular design; landscaping with native plants used by the Chumash for food, fiber, medi- cine, or ceremonials; a passive- solar-heated exhibit building; and a demonstration village, a contin- ually evolving settle- ment where visitors will work with Native

Parrot feathers from Mexico were traded to the Chumash

American Indians in tra- ditional crafts. Volunteers and donations are wel- come for all of these projects. A temporary exhibit and information building on the site is open Sundays from 10 A.M. to 5 P.M.

A network of trails fans across the hills of Rancho Sierra Vista/Satwiwa. The 1.5- mile **Satwiwa Loop Trail** is a gentle walk through the grasslands and coastal sage chaparral of the Satwiwa Native American Indian Natural Area. Guided hikes on the trail are offered. An offshoot trail heads east, down to the creek in the deep upper Sycamore Canyon and a series of small falls in a lush riparian forest graced with giant ferns. This trail ulti- mately leads to Tri-Peaks in Point Mugu State Park.

31 Red Rock Canyon Park

Location: Stunt Road, Calabasas; see map page vii

Administered by: Santa Monica Mountains Conservancy
(310) 456-5046
(800) 533-PARK

Hours: Sunrise to sunset

Fees: No entrance fees

Facilities: Chemical toilets (wheelchair accessible), water, picnic tables

Parking: Limited street parking

FYI: Dogs must be on leash. Alcohol, firearms, motor vehicles, fires, and camping are prohibited.

Let your imagination run as your feet explore the maze of giant, fantastically eroded boulders at Red Rock Canyon Park. Shallow caves and overhangs in the sandstone and conglomerate rocks offer hiding places and shady retreats from a hot summer day. Chaparral predominates in this secluded side canyon to Topanga Canyon. The conservancy has renovated a pre-existing building there, converting it from a Boy Scouts of America facility to a wilderness training and educational center.

32 Rocky Oaks

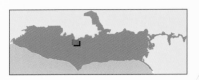

Location: Mulholland Highway, Agoura Hills; see map page vi

Administered by: National Park Service (818) 597-9192, ext. 201

Hours: Open twenty-four hours

Fees: No entrance fee

Facilities: Chemical toilets

Parking: Free NPS lot; open 8 A.M. to sunset

FYI: Firearms, motor vehicles, fires, and camping are prohibited. Dogs must be on leash.

A pond surrounded by grassy meadows; a dense, shady grove of coast live oak trees; and scenic boulder-strewn ramparts make Rocky Oaks one of the most pleasant picnic sites in the central Santa Monica Mountains.

At the junction of Mulholland Highway and Kanan Road, Rocky Oaks was homesteaded around the turn of the century. In the 1950s and 1960s, Vernon and Heriott Brown further developed this then-remote site, planting orchards, farming the grasslands, and building the pond to water their cattle. The pond usually has water except in drought

Coast live oak

years, making it one of the few places in these hills where ducks and other waterfowl can be found.

You'll find many picnic tables scattered in the grove of oaks and a few exotic Deodar cedars, as well as a small amphitheater. Gentle well-graded trails lead through the meadow, and connect with a hillside network of loop trails that offers views of the surrounding valley at the head of Zuma Canyon. A few small caves and a spring surrounded by willows and sycamores are nestled in the rocks at the west edge of the park, with dense scrub oak chaparral mixed with California bay trees on the slope above.

33 Santa Monica Municipal Pier

Location: Pacific Coast Highway and Santa Monica Freeway, Santa Monica; see map page viii

Administered by: Pier Restoration Corporation
(310) 458-8900, Pier office

Hours: Open twenty-four hours

Fees: No entrance fee

Facilities: Restrooms, water, restaurants, food concessions, playground, amusement park

Parking: Paid parking on the pier and in adjacent beach lot to the north

FYI: Be sure to see the antique carousel and its hand-carved wooden horses.

For an afternoon of classic family entertainment, visit the Santa Monica Pier, the last of the many great amusement piers that were strung like pearls along the southern California coast in the early 1900s. Ocean breezes and vivid sunsets will soothe you as

marionettes, jugglers, and other sidewalk performers entertain. When hunger strikes, dine at one of several pubs and restaurants, or snack on hot dogs, cotton candy, or fried fish.

The pier's world-famous restored antique carousel—with forty-four hand-carved wooden horses—and its building were used to depict a 1920s Chicago scene in the filming of the movie, The Sting, starring Robert Redford and Paul Newman. The playground at nearby Carousel Park, with a giant waterspray-breathing dragon, offers quieter

diversions for children. A fish market sells fresh fish, but you may prefer to catch the fish yourself from the pier's lower deck, one of the better angling spots on Santa Monica Bay; you can buy bait and tackle on the pier. Bonito, mackerel, rock cod, and even halibut are caught from this pier.

Beginning in the 1830s, cargo was landed here at what was known as Shoo Fly Landing; in the 1870s, this included tar from the La Brea tar pits destined for construction projects in booming San Francisco. In 1875, Nevada Senator John P. Jones built a 1,740-foot wharf to receive cargo for the construction of his Los Angeles & Independence Railroad; this line was intended to link Santa Monica with Los Angeles and Salt Lake City. The line was eventually absorbed in competition with Collis Huntington, of the dominant Southern Pacific Railway, and the wharf was demolished in 1879. In 1892, Huntington revived hopes for a giant breakwater and harbor at Santa Monica, to be named Port Los Angeles, and built the 4,720-foot Long Wharf, but in 1896, San Pedro finally won out over the bay city in its battle for federal sanctions, and became the region's major port.

Part of the current pier, known as the Pleasure Pier, was built in 1908, and is combined with the Santa Monica pier, built in 1920. It gained international renown with the construction of the first of three successive carousels, the now-defunct fifty-mile-an-hour Blue Streak Roller Coaster, and with the opening of the La Monica Ballroom in 1924. On its opening night in the 1930s, at the height of the pier's popularity, this elegant building, with its Arabian Nights-inspired design, drew fifty thousand people. Currently, plans are in progress for a Fun Zone, complete with rides, games, and food concessions, bringing back the excitement of days past.

34 Santa Monica State Beach

Location: Pacific Coast Highway, Santa Monica; see map page viii

Administered by: City of Santa Monica for the California Department of Parks and Recreation
(310) 458-8310 or 458-8689

Hours: Open twenty-four hours

Fees: No entrance fee

Facilities: Restrooms, water, playground, volleyball nets, gymnastic equipment, restaurants and food concessions; bicycle rentals, ball playing (in designated areas only)

Parking: Paid parking lots

FYI: Alcohol, firearms, fireworks, motor vehicles, bicycles, glass containers, percussion instruments, fires, camping, dogs, and horses are prohibited.

Like a year-round party, the circuslike scene at Santa Monica State Beach is at the heart of the California fitness sun-and-fun culture. Glamorous and colorful people abound here, engaged in seemingly nonstop volleyball, roller blading, boogie boarding, surfing, bicycling, swimming, and sunbathing.

This broad, white, sandy beach, the most popular on the West Coast, officially extends from Chatauqua Boulevard on the north to Venice City Beach on the south, a distance of about three miles. The palm-lined **South Bay Bicycle Trail** with parallel walking path replaces the beachfront boardwalk built here in the early 1900s and guides you along the waterfront from Will Rogers State Beach to Torrance, a total of 20.3 miles. Bicycle rentals are available at several points along the path.

Surfing and bodysurfing the long beach break are popular here. You can wade farther out at this shallow beach than at most other beaches in the area, but beware of bad rip currents; swim and surf only in front of a staffed lifeguard tower.

North of the Santa Monica Municipal Pier, the beach closely parallels Pacific Coast Highway at the foot of the bluffs in Palisades Park; climb the stairs for a sunset view of the bay. This area was the original "Muscle Beach," named first for mussels on the pier, but later for the many athletes, gymnasts, and Hollywood-hopeful weightlifters working out here during the Depression and after.

Beach-trolley parties became the rage beginning in the 1890s and started Santa Monica's era of fun in the sun. Giant bath houses sprang up along the beach, including the North Beach Bath House with its huge, heated indoor saltwater pool and one hundred porcelain-lined tubs, and its successor, the exclusive Deauville, with a French-medieval exterior and private, glass-covered beach. Counterpart to the bath houses were the many great pleasure piers along the bayfront, including, among others, the Crystal Pier, the Million Dollar Pier, Ocean Park Pier (Pacific Ocean Park, or POP), and the Lick Pier (home of the famed Aragon Ballroom, broadcast home of Lawrence Welk in the 1950s). The only one that remains is the Santa Monica Municipal Pier.

The beachfront was a glamour center beginning in the 1920s, and became known as "Rolls Royce Row" when the likes of Cary Grant and Mary Pickford (with Douglas Fairbanks) had luxury homes built here. Most notable among these was the massive estate built for silent-film star Marion Davies by William Randolph Hearst.

35 Solstice Canyon Park

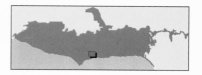

Location: Corral Canyon Road, Malibu; see map page vi

Administered by: Santa Monica Mountains Conservancy
(310) 456-5046
(800) 533-PARK

Hours: 8 A.M. to 5 P.M. winter; 8 A.M. to 6 P.M. summer

Fees: No individual entrance fee; $5/car, $40/bus fee

Facilities: Chemical toilet, water, picnic tables, book and map sales

Parking: Paid parking at visitor center parking lot. Do not park on Corral Canyon Road.

FYI: Dogs must be on leash. Alcohol, firearms, motor vehicles, fires, and camping are prohibited.

Solstice Canyon is one of the very few canyons along the Santa Monica Mountains coast that harbors a perennial stream.

You can experience an uninterrupted transition from ocean to mountains by following a creek-side trail from Corral/Dan Blocker State Beach to the Solstice Canyon parking lot off Corral Canyon Road. From here, hikers, mountain bikers, and equestrians may follow the paved Old Solstice Road into the interior; it is a leisurely 1.5 miles to Tropical Terrace, deep in this sheltered pastoral canyon. This is one of the finest and easiest bicycle trips in the mountains, and can also be traveled by energetic people in wheelchairs and families with strollers.

Raptors such as great horned owls and red-shouldered and red-tailed hawks may be seen roosting in the white alders, California bay trees, giant sycamores and live oaks that hang over the stream.

Bobcat

One live oak, known as the **Keller Family Oak**, has a circumference of eighteen feet. Away from the stream, mixed chaparral, black walnut, and live oak stands alternate with grassy meadows that offer excellent spring wildflowers. Bobcats and deer inhabit the canyon.

Two picnic areas in the canyon offer tables, chemical toilets, and shaded meadows for relaxing. A short way up the canyon, you will find a visitor center where you may buy books and maps and obtain information; trail information is available in five Pacific Rim languages. You'll find other interesting and historical buildings in the canyon. On the side of the canyon a mile up the trail is a bizarre fifty-foot-high cylindrical building with a conical roof that was used from 1961 to 1973 by Thomson-Ramo-Woolridge, Inc.

(TRW) to test a device made to calibrate satellite payload instrumentation. The site was chosen because it was remote from manmade and natural magnetic disturbances. The TRW building now houses the offices of the Santa Monica Mountains Conservancy.

High on the hillside above the TRW building is a private residence of striking design; it juts precipitously into space as though being launched and is but one example of the extravagant and imaginative architecture increasingly found in the Santa Monica Mountains.

About one mile from the parking lot on the east side of the creek is a much more humble structure, the **Matthew Keller cabin**, built around 1865 of river cobbles. It was Don Mateo Keller who in 1864 finally succeeded in obtaining a perfected title from the U.S. Land Commission to the thirteen-thousand-acre Spanish land grant Rancho Topanga Malibu Sequit, which encompassed all of present-day Malibu and then some. The stone cabin was a summer home for the Kellers, who needed a full day to travel to the canyon from Santa Monica. In those days before the coastal roads, they could only make the trip during low tides that allowed them to squeeze their buggy past rock outcrops on the beach. Today, the restored Keller cabin is used as housing for park employees.

At the end of the paved trail is the **Tropical Terrace**, the remains of the home of Fred and Florence Roberts, from whom the canyon was purchased for park use. Built in the 1950s, the home was featured in *Architectural Digest* and *Home Magazine*. Around the ranch-style home were built elaborate stone terraces and stream-fed fish ponds shaded by date palms, bamboo, philodendron, bird-of-paradise, and ivy-laced pines. The house burned in a 1982 fire and the grounds were further ravaged by subsequent floods, but the ruins invite exploration and dreams of what it would be like to live in such an idyllic setting. Picnicking on the stone courtyard is a delight, as is exploring the adjacent **Grotto Waterfalls**, with their series of cascades and rock pools, and the ruins of stone stairs.

From the terraces, hikers may follow the 2.6-mile **Sostomo Loop Trail** that heads farther upstream and then climbs steeply to loop across the east-facing slope of the canyon; good views of the Pacific can be had here. Another choice is the 1.8-mile **Rising Sun Trail**, which switchbacks steeply up the west-facing slope and then descends gradually to the visitor center.

36 Tapia Park

Location: Las Virgenes Road, Calabasas; see map page vii

Administered by: California Department of Parks and Recreation (818) 880-0350

Hours: Sunrise to sunset

Fees: No entrance fee

Facilities: Chemical toilet, water, picnic tables, barbecue grills, dirt baseball diamond, basketball court

Parking: Free off-street lots; bus parking

FYI: Alcohol, firearms, motor vehicles, bicycles, fires, camping, and dogs are prohibited.

Giant live oak trees and grassy meadows, extensive shaded picnic grounds, ball courts, and adjacent natural areas make Tapia Park a favorite destination for large family groups and organized groups from the city. With easy access, just five miles down the Malibu Canyon-Las Virgenes Road from U.S. 101, the park is especially busy on weekends, when it resembles a neighborhood block party. Weekdays allow quieter relaxation.

The park offers a baseball diamond and basketball court. Walk-in picnicking is allowed in the back side of the park, where Malibu Creek runs through a grove of sycamores and dense willow thickets. Next door are the Mountain Crags Camp administered by the Salvation Army and the L.A. County Probation Department's Camp David Gilmore.

From the northwest corner of the park, the .9-mile **Tapia Spur Trail** leads into a Malibu Creek State Park campground. From the junction of Piuma Road and Malibu Canyon Road, the **Backbone Trail** heads southeasterly through a lush riparian woodland of cottonwoods and willows, then runs easterly high on the ridge toward Stunt Road.

The park is named for José Bartolomé Tapia, a member of the 1773 expedition of Juan Bautista de Anza. In 1804, Tapia was the first European to be granted "ownership" of Rancho Topanga Malibu Sequit, a vast area that included most of the Santa Monica Mountains and the Malibu Coast.

37 Temescal Canyon Park

Location: Pacific Coast Highway, Pacific Palisades; see map page viii

Administered by: Los Angeles City Department of Recreation and Parks (310) 837-8116

Hours: 6 A.M. to 10 P.M.

Fees: No entrance fee

Facilities: Restroom, water, picnic tables

Parking: On-street parking only

FYI: Alcohol, firearms, motor vehicles, fires, camping, and horses are prohibited. Dogs must be on leash.

Immediately up the hill from Will Rogers State Beach, Temescal Canyon Park in Pacific Palisades extends for about a mile along both sides of Temescal Canyon Road. Picnic and playground facilities and large, well-groomed lawns make this a popular destination for family and small-group outings. Ramadas, sycamores, and spreading coral trees (named for their brilliant red blossoms) shade visitors from the summer sun.

38 Temescal Gateway Park

Location: Sunset Boulevard, Pacific Palisades; see map page viii

Administered by: Santa Monica Mountains Conservancy (310) 456-5046 (800) 533-PARK

Hours: Sunrise to sunset

Fees: No entrance fee

Facilities: Restrooms, water, picnic facilities

Parking: Free off-street parking; no parking on the beach

FYI: Dogs are allowed on leash in Gateway but are not allowed in adjoining Topanga State Park. Bicycles prohibited on trails. Alcohol, firearms, motor vehicles, fires, camping, and horses are prohibited.

Named for the Spanish word for the sweathouses of the native Tongva/Gabrieliños, Temescal Gateway Park (dedicated in May 1994) is the main southern entrance and parking area for hikers heading into the steep, brushy backcountry of Topanga State Park. One trail travels up Temescal Canyon before steeply ascending Temescal Ridge; an alternate route leaves directly from Gateway Park to climb the western ridge.

The canyon is densely shaded by live oaks, sycamores, and—in the lower reaches—exotic eucalyptus. Upstream, the creek generally runs year round, tumbling over several waterfalls. Temescal Canyon owes its undeveloped status to the Presbyterian Church, which, beginning in the 1920s, preserved the canyon as a site for their annual Chatauqua summer festivals of religious and secular instruction, athletic competition, music, and singing.

39 Topanga State Beach

40 Topanga State Park

Location: Pacific Coast Highway, Malibu; see map page viii

Administered by: Los Angeles County Beaches and Harbors
(310) 305-9503

Hours: 6 A.M. to sunset

Fees: No entrance fee

Facilities: Restroom, water, cold showers

Parking: Paid parking lot on bluff, handicap-accessible parking below

FYI: Alcohol, firearms, motor vehicles, bicycles, horses, rubber inflatable flotation devices, jet skis, and boat launching are prohibited.

Location: Entrada Road, Topanga; see map page viii

Administered by: California Department of Parks and Recreation
(310) 455-2465

Hours: Open twenty-four hours

Fees: Parking fee is day-use fee at Trippet Ranch and Dead Horse lot; self-pay overnight camping at Musch Ranch Camp

Facilities: Restrooms, water, picnic tables, camping

Parking: Paid parking lot open 8 A.M. to 7 P.M. summer; 8 A.M. to 5 P.M. winter

FYI: Dogs are not allowed on trails. Firearms, motor vehicles, and open fires are prohibited. Alcohol prohibited in Santa Ynez Canyon.

Prized by surfers for its offering of a rare point break, Topanga State Beach is considered by many to be the second-best surfing area in the L.A. area (only the Malibu Surfrider surpasses it). The surf is best in the summer, when southern swells hit this part of the coast. Nonsurfers enjoy the mile-long, wide, sandy beach for sunbathing, but most find the sea bottom too cobbled for good swimming, and a steep shore break limits body surfing. There is a small sunbathing area with a catamaran landing just east of the Charthouse Restaurant. Trees at the beach's edge afford a few shady picnic sites, and Topanga Creek flows impressively after winter rains. Tidepool creatures can be seen at low tide on the cobbled point.

Wild and rugged Topanga State Park, featuring high, boulder-studded ridges, canyons clothed in dense chaparral, and hidden streamside forests, offers ample getaway opportunities for hikers, riders, and bikers right at the doorstep of metropolitan Los Angeles. In fact, most of the park's ten thousand acres are within the Los Angeles city limits, making this the largest park of its type in North America and doubling its importance as a protector of air quality. The scenic relief

Hermit crab

from urban life that it offers also cannot be underestimated.

Topanga is a Tongva/Gabrieliño term believed to mean "the place where the mountains meet the sea." This is thought to have been a kind of "joint use" area, where the Tongva/Gabrieliños and the Chumash peacefully coexisted. These two groups differed in religion, language, and social organization, but shared virtually the same material culture.

Day use and trails: Picnic sites in a live oak grove are located near park headquarters at Trippet Ranch in Topanga Canyon. Here, at the park's small visitor center, you can see exhibits on local natural history and obtain information from park volunteers.

The park has thirty-two miles of roads and trails and five major entrances, plus several more obscure ones. Mountain bikes are allowed on the eighteen miles of fire roads, and horses are permitted on all trails except one.

Four trails begin near Trippet Ranch: the **Nature Trail**, a 1 mile, self-guided loop; **Dead Horse Trail**, 1.1 miles to a small parking lot (restrooms available) on Entrada Road; **Musch Ranch Trail**, .9 mile to the Musch Ranch Camp, then 1.1 miles to Eagle Junction. The **East Topanga Fire Road** is reached by a short climb from the ranch to a high ridgeline; follow it 1.1 miles north to Eagle Junction, or 3 miles south to Parker Mesa Overlook.

The **Santa Ynez Canyon Trail** runs 1.5 miles from the East Topanga Fire Road down to the canyon bottom, then 1.1 miles up the fern-lined canyon shaded by oaks and sycamores to a stone alcove carved by a fifteen-foot waterfall. Easier access to the

canyon is gained from Avenida de la Montura, near the end of Palisades Drive. **Eagle Rock/ Eagle Spring Trail**, a 2.6-mile fire-road loop from Eagle Junction, is one of the park's most popular destinations.

The "**Hub**," a popular meeting place for backcountry travelers, is the junction of four trails: the Eagle Rock and Eagle Springs trails; the **Temescal Fire Road/Fire Road 30**; and the **Temescal Fire Road/Temescal Ridge Trail**. A chemical toilet is located at the Hub.

About a quarter mile south of the Hub is Cathedral Rock, a sandstone *massif* (an elevated block of old, complex rocks) riddled with caves and hollows; it offers breathtaking views into upper Rustic Canyon.

Rogers Trail, the westernmost section of the Backbone Trail, is 6.6 miles long and ends at Will Rogers State Historic Park.

Camping: Musch Ranch Camp is one of only two backcountry camps in the Santa Monica Mountains. It can be eight individual sites **or** one group site (maximum twenty-five people), water, restrooms, picnic tables, and corrals. A self-pay fee area, it is first-come, first-served. There is no motorized vehicle access; it can be reached by foot or horseback only, via Musch Ranch Trail from Trippet Ranch. The bicycle entry is off Hillside Trail Road via the fire road. No dogs are allowed in camp, and no smoking, open fires, or wood gathering are permitted; gas stoves are allowed. Bicycles are permitted only on designated fire roads.

Backcountry areas may be evacuated and closed to entry during periods of high fire danger; call (805) 488-8147 for fire information.

41 Upper Franklin Canyon/Sooky Goldman Nature Center

Location: Franklin Canyon Road, Beverly Hills; see map page ix

Administered by: Mountains Education Program
(310) 858-3090

Hours: Sunrise to sunset

Fees: No entrance fee

Facilities: Restrooms, water, picnic tables, auditorium, amphitheater

Parking: Free parking

FYI: Dogs must be on leash. Alcohol, firearms, motor vehicles, bicycles, smoking, swimming, fishing, fires, camping, and horses are prohibited.

Upper Franklin Canyon contains a variety of plant communities and is home to local wildlife ranging from rabbits and woodrats to deer and bobcat. Upper Franklin Reservoir, formerly a water source for part of Los Angeles, is now a stopover on the California flyway for migratory birds and a good place to see birds year-round. There are a number of nature trails, including a **trail for the blind and handicapped** by Heavenly Pond. This trail follows a wheelchair-accessible cement walkway and has signs in braille and standard signs interpreting native plants and animals.

Franklin Canyon houses the Sooky Goldman Nature Center. The William O. Douglas Outdoor Classroom (WODOC), operated by the Mountains Education Program, offers docent-led programs for elementary school groups on weekday mornings. Other docents lead walks for the public on weekends and a variety of programs, including "Birding for Beginners," "Babes in the Woods," "Photo Fun," and "T'ai Chi Walk." All of WODOC's programs—including those that train individuals to be docents—are free.

42 Ventura County Beaches/County Line Beach

Location: Pacific Coast Highway, Ventura; see map pages iv–v

Administered by: California Department of Parks and Recreation
(818) 880-0350

Hours: Open twenty-four hours

Fees: None

Facilities: Restrooms, water, picnic tables, hot and cold showers

Parking: Limited free parking on Pacific Coast Highway; no parking between 10 P.M. to 5 A.M.

FYI: Alcohol, camping, firearms, motor vehicles, bicycles, fires, and horses are prohibited. Dogs must be on leash.

A series of narrow, rocky beaches extend from the Ventura County line to the mouth of Deer Creek Canyon. Fishing, beachcombing, and birdwatching are favored activities here.

The cobbled point at County Line Beach, near the junction of Highway 1 (Pacific Coast Highway) and Yerba Buena Road, is a popular surfing location. A small sandy beach lies to the east.

Desert cottontail

 43 Wilacre Park

 44 Will Rogers State Beach

Location: Fryman Road, Beverly Hills; see map page ix

Administered by: Santa Monica Mountains Conservancy
(310) 456-5046
(800) 533-PARK

Hours: Sunrise to sunset

Fees: No entrance fee

Facilities: None

Parking: Limited free street parking

FYI: Alcohol, firearms, motor vehicles, bicycles, fires, camping, and horses are prohibited.

Location: Pacific Coast Highway, Pacific Palisades; see map page viii

Administered by: Los Angeles County Beaches and Harbors
(310) 305-9503

Hours: Summer, 6 A.M. to 10 P.M.; winter, 6 A.M. to 8 P.M.

Fees: No entrance fee

Facilities: Restroom, water, picnic tables

Parking: Paid parking at 14800 Pacific Coast Highway (139 spaces); 15800 Pacific Coast Highway (1,383 spaces); 17700 Pacific Coast Highway (58 spaces)

FYI: Alcohol, firearms, motor vehicles, bicycles, glass containers, inner tubes, boat launching, jet skis, barbecues, fires, camping, dogs, and horses are prohibited.

Once the home of Will Acres, a renowned silent film star cowboy, Wilacre Park is today an island of open, grassy land in the midst of suburban Studio City. At the junction of Laurel Canyon Boulevard and Fryman Road, the park offers good examples of walnut woodlands mixed with toyon and ceanothus. A trail ascends a ridgeline with good views of the eastern San Fernando Valley, and connects with the **Dearing Mountain Trail** from Coldwater Canyon Park and Fryman Canyon Overlook. A loop may be made from the latter by following Fryman Road.

This beach is named for the internationally famed humorist Will Rogers, actor, radio star, and columnist, whose home in the hills nearby is preserved as a state park. Will Rogers State Beach has for decades been heavily used by the movie industry because of its wide, white-sand expanses and convenient access to Hollywood and Burbank. It's also a favorite hang-out for actors, extras, and Hollywood "wannabes," and a preferred destination for inland residents escaping the valley heat. The parking lots fill early on summer weekends.

The beach's popularity dates back to the 1860s, when the area was in the hands of the Reyes and Marquez families, heirs to Spanish land grants that included much of Santa Monica and Malibu. Tent cities sprang up on the beach and in groves of sycamores in adjacent

Ceanothus

Santa Monica Canyon (just north of San Vicente Boulevard); resort hotels followed. Around the turn of the century, Santa Monica Canyon's rowdy saloons, bawdy-houses, dance halls, and shanty-towns became the target of a temperance and reform movement led by Malibu land baron Frederick Rindge. Later, beach-front squatter shacks gave way to cottages built by Hollywood stars.

The ocean here warms up to around sixty-five degrees F. by May or June, and to sixty-eight to seventy degrees, July through September. Although there's plenty of white sand for sun-bathing, the beach is a bit rocky in the surf zone. Two cautions: because the water deepens and waves break close to shore, swim-mers and body surfers are in dan-ger of being slammed down on the sand. Also on occasion, larger "sneaker" waves occur around the beach's series of rock *groynes* (small jettys extending from shore, intended to prevent beach ero-sion). Surfing is not allowed on most of the beach during busy times; look for the black-ball flag at lifeguard towers, which indicates no surfing or windsurfing. Boogie boards are allowed at all times.

Rockfalls are frequent from the steep *alluvium* (sand and mud deposited by flowing water) cliffs across the Pacific Coast Highway. Cliff-top homes here are gradually losing support as erosion continues, and more than one balcony has collapsed. Just south of Temescal Canyon, near the point at which the Santa Monica Fault crosses unseen under the high-way, the road has been routed around the foot of a giant cliff slump dating from 1958.

Will Rogers State Beach offers possibilities for good surf fishing for perch, California corbina, bonito, and halibut. The **South**

Bay Bicycle Trail extends along the beach twenty miles from here south to Torrance. Abundant vol-leyball courts make Will Rogers State Beach a center for the young and athletic.

45 Will Rogers State Historic Park

Location: Sunset Boulevard, Pacific Palisades; see map page viii

Administered by: California Department of Parks and Recreation (310) 454-8212

Hours: 8 A.M. to 6 P.M. House closed on Thanksgiving, Christmas, and New Year's Day

Fees: No entrance fee

Facilities: Restrooms, water, picnic tables, polo field, stables

Parking: Paid parking

FYI: Firearms, motor vehicles, fires, barbecues, and camping are prohib-ited. Dogs must be on leash. Bicycles allowed on paved roads and loop trail.

In 1928, Will Rogers built a ranch home in the hills above Santa Monica. Here he spent his last years writing, riding, roping, and entertaining friends. With the addition of a second story, what began as a weekend getaway "cabin" became the south wing and guest quar-ters of the pres-ent house. Will needed the high-beamed ceilings and open space of the cabin's living room for his roping practice.

In defense against his roping habit, friends gave him a stuffed calf to keep themselves out of the lasso. The well-worn calf remains today, along with an extensive display of furnishings and memorabilia from Will's life, testifying to his love of the Southwest and respect for his Native American Indian ancestry.

Betty Rogers left the property to the state at her death in 1944, with two conditions: change nothing in the house and allow polo every Saturday and Sunday. Will was an avid polo fan, and the eucalyptus-ringed polo field in front of his cabin still rings with matches every weekend (weather permitting) and hosts the annual competition for the Will Rogers Memorial Trophy. This is a fine spot for an elegant picnic on the lawn, but on Sundays you may find yourself turned away due to crowds and limited parking.

Will was constantly planting trees and shrubs around the property, building fences and roping and riding rings, or carving new riding trails into the surrounding hills. One of these is the **Inspiration Point Trail**, a two-mile loop fire road that leads to an overlook with outstanding views of the house and grounds, the palatial estates on adjoining properties, the city of Santa Monica, and the Palos Verdes Peninsula. This is the eastern

terminus of the uncompleted Backbone Trail, which leads steadily up the ridge into the wild

heart of Topanga State Park, passing nearly pure stands of big pod ceanothus on the way.

46 Zuma Beach County Park/ Westward Beach

Location: Pacific Coast Highway, Malibu; see map page vi

Administered by: Los Angeles County Beaches and Harbors
(310) 305-9503

Hours: 6 A.M. to midnight

Fees: No entrance fee

Facilities: Restrooms, water, picnic tables, cold showers, volleyball courts, playground

Parking: Paid parking lot; free street parking on Westward Beach Road and Pacific Coast Highway

FYI: Alcohol, firearms, motor vehicles, bicycles, glass containers, fires, camping, dogs, and horses are prohibited.

When the southland bakes on a hot summer day, tens of thousands of residents of the San Fernando and other inland valleys seek relief at Zuma Beach County Park and Westward Beach. These

Grunion

two and one-half miles of broad, sandy beach—largest on the Malibu coast—invite sunbathing, swimming, surfing, volleyball, and other beach sports.

Zuma and Westward beaches form the first major stretch of beach to the west of Point Dume and outside of Santa Monica Bay. This location means that the water is cleaner and clearer here than at most Los Angeles area

Santa Monica Bay, Zuma Beach, and Point Dume

beaches, but also colder and often more hazardous, with rough surf and large and more-frequent rip currents. Nevertheless, the area is considered one of the safest because of its intensive lifeguard service; about one thousand rescues a year are made at Zuma alone. As at all county-operated beaches, swim only in front of a staffed lifeguard tower.

Surfing is allowed until 11 A.M., with the area in front of Lifeguard Tower Twelve reserved for surfing at all times. The beach is host to the Annual Skimboard Championships. Catamarans may be launched at the west end with a permit. Surf fishers catch corbina, surfperch, halibut, and opaleye here, and in the summer, the beaches host nighttime grunion-spawning runs following full or new moons. Nearby Point Dume State Beach is popular for sunbathing, swimming, scuba diving, and surf fishing.

47 Zuma Canyon/ Trancas Canyon

Location: Near Zuma Beach, Malibu; see map page vi

Administered by: National Park Service (818) 597-9192, ext. 201

Hours: Open twenty-four hours

Fees: No entrance fee

Facilities: Water at Bonsall Drive trailhead

Parking: Free NPS lots

FYI: Bicycles allowed only on Zuma Ridge, Zuma Edison, and Backbone trails. Firearms, motor vehicles, fires, and camping are prohibited. Dogs must be on leash.

It seems hard to believe that the wild, remote, and rugged character of the Zuma Canyon-

Trancas Canyon complex remains essentially undisturbed less than twenty miles from metropolitan Los Angeles. But in this area, much of the land remains untrailed and untrammeled.

To reach the heart of this mountain empire, drive north on Pacific Coast Highway. Turn right at Busch, right on Rainsford, left on Bonsall Drive. Park at the National Park Service lot. The 1.4-mile hike from here up the streambed is level and easy, although you may encounter stream crossings in the rainy season and some rock-hopping is required toward the end. Grassy spots for picnics abound under sycamores and black walnut trees. Farther upstream, the riparian forest becomes more lush and the trail ends in a series of clear pools at the base of a rocky cliff.

Sheer rock faces and several waterfalls await the determined hiker in the upper reaches of Zuma Canyon. This area is without trails; travel through it requires considerable boulder-hopping. The best access is via Newton Canyon; park on Kanan Dume Road, about two miles south of Mulholland Highway.

The steep gorge of neighboring Trancas Canyon to the west is on par with upper Zuma, and offers fine waterfalls of its own. This area has no trails and is not for the faint of heart. The best access point is from a pullout on Encinal Canyon Road, two miles west of the junction with Mulholland Highway and just east of the Malibu Conservation Camp.

When you're ready to head for the high country for outstanding views of the Pacific and the wild canyons, follow the **Zuma Ridge Trail** (Zuma Motorway). This fire road (closed to motorized vehicles) is well-graded but steep at its southern end. It is 5.9 miles from the end of Busch Drive in Malibu to Encinal Canyon Road. Determined mountain bikers can make a long loop trip by going up Zuma Ridge and down Kanan Dume Road.

Zuma Canyon Trail begins at the end of Bonsall Drive in Malibu, off Pacific Coast Highway. The **southern Zuma Ridge trailhead** is at the end of Busch Drive in Malibu; turn right on Busch Drive off Pacific Coast Highway. Follow Busch Drive until it ends at an unpaved parking lot. From the parking lot go straight for the Zuma Ridge trailhead, turn right for Zuma Canyon Trail.

Part III

Using the Parks

To ensure preservation for future generations, all natural, cultural, and historical features, including plants, animals, rocks, and historic artifacts (such as arrowheads), are protected by law. Do not remove, disturb, or deface them. Hunting or killing any animal—including rattlesnakes—is prohibited. In addition, each area has specific regulations. These regulations are usually posted at the site or listed in informational handouts provided by the park.

Administering Agencies

California Department
of Parks and Recreation
1925 Las Virgenes Rd.
Calabasas, CA 91302
(818) 880-0350

City of Malibu Parks and Recreation
23555 Civic Center Way
Malibu, CA 90265
(310) 456-5190

City of Santa Monica
Parks and Sports
2600 Ocean Park Blvd.
Santa Monica, CA 90405
(310) 458-8974

City of Santa Monica
Manager of Economic Development
3223 Donald Douglass Loop S.
Santa Monica, CA 90404
(310) 458-8712

City of Santa Monica
Cultural Affairs
1855 Main St.
Santa Monica, CA 90401
(310) 458-8555

Commanding Officer
NAVAIRWPNSTA
521 9th St.
Pt. Mugu, CA 93042-5001
(805) 989-1110

County of Ventura Parks
800 S. Victoria
Ventura, CA 93009-1030
(805) 654-3951

J. Paul Getty Museum
P.O. Box 2112
Santa Monica, CA 90407-2112
(310) 459-7611

Los Angeles City Department of
Recreation and Parks
Public Relations
200 N. Main St., 13th Floor
City Hall East
Los Angeles, CA 90012
(213) 485-5555

Los Angeles County
Beaches and Harbors
13837 Fiji Way
Marina Del Rey, CA 90292
(310) 305-9503

Mountains Education Program
2600 Franklin Canyon
Beverly Hills, CA 90210
(310) 858-3090

Mountains Restoration Trust
24955 Pacific Coast Highway,
Ste. 301
Malibu, CA 90265
(310) 456-5625

National Park Service
Santa Monica Mountains National
Recreation Area
30401 Agoura Rd.
Agoura Hills, CA 91301
(818) 597-9192

Pier Restoration Corporation
200 Santa Monica Pier, Suite A
Santa Monica, CA 90401
(310) 458-8900

Santa Monica Mountains Conservancy
Mountains Conservancy Foundation
3700 Solstice Canyon
Malibu, CA 90265
(310) 456-5046

TreePeople
12601 Mulholland Dr.
Beverly Hills, CA 90210
(818) 753-4600

Photo previous page: Backbone Trail, Malibu Creek State Park

Visitor Tips, Regulations

Private property
Private property mixes with public parklands throughout the mountains and beaches. Remember that many public lands and rights-of-way have been created only with the generous cooperation of private property owners. Be a good neighbor to private-property owners by respecting all postings and boundaries, maintaining quiet, and leaving all gates as you find them, whether open or closed.

Dogs in the parks
Dogs are permitted on leash in national park and Santa Monica Mountains Conservancy lands except as posted, and are allowed on leash at some beaches; check signs or call ahead.

Remember that other park visitors are unlikely to love your pet as much as you do. Keep your dog on a six-foot leash at all times, do not allow persistent barking, and be sure to clean up after your pet. Never take dogs inside buildings or tie them outside restrooms. If you leave your dog in your vehicle, be sure to provide adequate ventilation, especially when it's warm; temperatures inside a parked car can quickly rise high enough to cause heat stroke and even death.

On state park lands, dogs are permitted in developed public-use areas such as auto-accessible picnic areas and most campgrounds, but prohibited in the back-country. Dogs must be inside your tent or car at night.

Shooting and firearms
Shooting is prohibited except at established shooting ranges, and possession of loaded firearms, air rifles, or other weapons is prohibited on all park lands.

Fires and fireworks
Fires are prohibited except in designated campgrounds and picnic grounds; you must confine fires to stoves and fire rings provided or use a portable camp stove. Fireworks are prohibited.

Fire closures
To protect both the visitors and the area, park lands may periodically be closed to entry due to high fire danger. Watch for closure signs at major park entrances, and to be sure of the status, call (805) 488-8147 for fire closures in state parks, or (818) 597-9192, extension 201, for closures in National Park Service lands.

Smoking
Careless smokers are the main cause of brush fires in southern California. In conditions of extreme fire danger, smoking may be prohibited or restricted in some areas; inquire locally. Regardless of conditions, when you smoke, be sure to collect and carry out cigarette butts, since cigarette filters remain intact for decades when discarded on the ground. On National Park Service trails, you are required to stop and remain in one place while smoking.

Litter
If you pack it in, pack it out.

A well-equipped hiker

Noise

Most visitors go to our parklands to get away from the noise and aggravations of the city. Respect everyone's rights to quiet enjoyment by avoiding boisterous conduct and restricting the use of stereos.

Motor vehicles

Motor vehicles, including motorcycles and dirt bikes, must remain on designated roads and are prohibited on trails and fire roads.

Drivers with motor homes and trailers should inquire locally before driving on secondary roads.

Bicycling

Bicycles must never be ridden off roads and trails. Be sure the trails you plan to ride are open to you.

On national park lands, bicycles are permitted on unpaved roads and other trails as posted.

On state park lands, bicycles are permitted only on unpaved roads.

On highways, bicyclists should always ride single-file on the right-hand side of the road.

Restrict speed as visibility and trail conditions dictate. The speed limit in park lands is fifteen miles per hour.

Horses have the right of way. When encountering a horse, give warning and ask the rider if it is safe to pass, then proceed carefully. If necessary, stop and stand off to one side while they pass.

Horseback riding

Horses are permitted on most roads and trails except as posted; inquire at the park to be sure the trails you plan to ride are open to you. Horses are prohibited on all beaches and in most campgrounds and picnic areas.

The Backbone Trail

The idea of a continuous trail along the spine of the Santa Monica Mountains has been around for decades. On-the-ground surveys of potential routes for the trail began in 1983. The trail will be about sixty-five miles long, from Will Rogers State Historic Park to Point Mugu State Park. This will be the best opportunity for backpacking and extended hiking in the Santa Monicas.

The trail is being built by the various park management agencies, the Sierra Club, local trail councils, and hundreds of volunteers. Following is a list of some of the major sections of the trail already completed. See the individual park descriptions herein, or the *Guide to the Backbone Trail*, by Milt McAuley (1990, Canyon Publishing Company, Canoga Park, CA) for in-depth descriptions.

- Will Rogers State Historic Park to Trippet Ranch (Topanga State Park); 10 miles.
- Trippet Ranch to Saddle Peak via Topanga Meadows and Hondo Canyon; 7.9 miles.
- Saddle Peak to Tapia Park; 6.6 miles.
- Tapia Park to Latigo Canyon Road, via Malibu Creek State Park, Castro Crest (high and low routes); 9 to 11 miles.
- Latigo Canyon Road to Kanan Road at Newton Canyon; 2.1 miles.
- Zuma Canyon to Circle X Ranch at Yerba Buena Road (under construction); 12 miles.
- Yerba Buena Road to Danielson Multiuse Area (Circle X Ranch, Point Mugu State Park); 9.5 miles.
- Danielson Multiuse Area to Ray Miller Trailhead (Point Mugu State Park); 8 miles.

Communicate with passing hikers and bicyclists, letting them know how and when to pass. Let others know when you wish to pass, and do so on the left at a walk.

Avoid riding on steep or muddy trails, which can cause serious trail damage, and never take shortcuts.

If your horse is prone to kicking, tie a red flag on its tail when you're out riding.

Hiking

See the recommended reading list for guides detailing hikes throughout the recreation area.

Hike with one or more people when possible; this leaves someone to go for help if you encounter trouble.

Always tell someone at home where you are going and when you will be back.

When approached by a horse, stand quietly by the trail (all members of your party on the same side) until the horse has passed. If you overtake a horse and want to pass, ask the rider if it is safe, then proceed carefully. If the animal has a red flag on its tail, be aware that it is prone to kicking.

Stay on trails and know your limits.

Backcountry Hazards and Sanitation

Dehydration, heat stroke

Not drinking enough water while hiking in the mountains can cause dehydration, which can lead to heat stroke. Heat stroke is characterized by an extremely high body temperature—106 degrees or higher—and flushed, dry skin. Initial symptoms include dizziness, nausea, headache, and lack of perspiration. A wide-brim hat that covers the

top of your head, a thin cotton long-sleeve shirt, and long pants will reduce water loss and insulate you from extreme heat. Carry water and drink often. Drinking ample non-alcoholic fluids is essential to prevent heat stroke. For half-day or shorter hikes, carry at least one quart per person in the winter or two quarts in the summer; double for all-day hikes. Eating well is essential to provide the electrolytes needed to absorb water.

Hypothermia

Hypothermia is a lowered body temperature, and is caused by exposure to wind, water, or chilling from wet skin, as in a rainstorm. Contrary to popular belief, most cases occur at temperatures well above freezing. Untreated, severe hypothermia may rapidly cause death. Symptoms include confusion, lack of coordination, stumbling, sleepiness, fatigue, apathy, slurred speech, cold skin, blue skin, uncontrollable shivering (in early stages only), and unconsciousness.

Follow these precautions:

- Dress adequately. Wear a waterproof raincoat or poncho in the rain. Wear a hat and windproof outer clothing in the wind, with layers of wool or synthetic (not cotton) sweaters or shirts underneath; remove or add layers to adjust to temperature needs during exertion.
- Eat ample whole foods such as meat, nuts, bread, or cheese.
- Drink ample fluids, as much as three or four quarts per day when exercising. Avoid alcohol, as it accelerates heat and water loss.
- Pace yourself and do not become exhausted.
- Seek shelter when needed.
- Avoid prolonged periods of immersion in cold water, as when swimming, boating, or surfing.

Drinking water

Bring all the water you need for your backcountry excursions, and drink only from faucets in developed areas. Avoid immersing your head or swallowing water while swimming in ponds and creeks. No water can be relied on to be safe to drink, even that from mountain streams or springs. Water-borne bacteria, protozoa (such as *Giardia*), and viruses (such as hepatitis) are prevalent due to suburban and agricultural pollution; domestic animals, such as dogs and cattle; and improper sanitation practices by visitors.

For emergencies in the backcountry, be prepared to purify surface water with iodine tablets. These can be purchased ahead of time at most outdoor supply stores.

Sanitation

Where there are no bathrooms, help slow the trend toward increasing backcountry pollution by practicing proper sanitation.

Do your business at least two hundred feet from the nearest stream, pond, or spring. Bury solid waste in a six-inch-deep "cathole" dug with a stick or the heel of your boot; bacterial decomposition works fastest at this depth. Bring a sealable plastic bag and carry out all toilet paper; it will take months to decompose buried in the dry mountain soils, and much longer if left on the surface.

Fire conditions

Check on fire conditions before entering the backcountry. Brush fires spread with amazing speed in the mountain chaparral, especially when pushed by a Santa Ana or other high wind, and you could quickly be trapped and burned. Spend your time at the beach or other developed areas if danger is high. Don't smoke in the backcountry.

Poison oak

Watch for poison oak (it can be identified by its shiny, three-leaf clusters; learn to recognize it or carry a plant guide). Poison oak is most commonly found in moist areas such as streamside undergrowth, but can grow almost anywhere in chaparral. Contact with any part of the plant can cause severe skin eruptions and itching in most people. Wearing a long-sleeve shirt, long pants, and high socks will help protect you. Highly sensitive people

Poison oak

sometimes also wear gloves.

If you think you may have contacted the plant, on returning home:

- launder your clothes and wash yourself thoroughly with a strong soap such as castile;
- avoid excess scrubbing, as this may spread the oils;
- apply calamine or other first aid creams; and
- see your doctor.

Ticks

Inspect yourself for ticks. Ticks are brown to black, oval, eight-legged *arthropods* (a member of the same group as insects, spiders, and crustaceans). They can range from the size of a pinhead to the size of an apple seed. Several species live in the Santa Monica Mountains.

Mature ticks cling to brush and grass, waiting for a mammal (such as a deer or hiker) to brush against them. The tick then attaches itself to the host in a warm, dark place. Once attached, a tick bores its mouthparts into the host to suck blood. In the process of sucking, the tick can transmit organisms that can cause serious diseases. Ticks are most abundant in the spring but can be found any time of the year. Protect yourself from ticks by taking these precautions:

- Avoid going off trails.
- Wearing a light-color long-sleeve shirt and long pants will make it easier to spot ticks.
- Tuck your shirt tail into your pants, and your pant legs into your socks.
- Apply an insect repellent certified for use against ticks around your boots and pant legs.
- Have a partner regularly inspect you all around, before ticks have a chance to crawl into your clothes. Flick ticks off with a stick or stone; touching them can transmit disease organisms.
- Check yourself thoroughly when you get back from a hike. Inspect your head and the rest of your body while showering or in front of a mirror.
- Don't take pets into the brush or backcountry, and be sure to inspect them thoroughly when you finish your hike.

If you find a tick attached,

- grasp it with a small pointed tweezer close to the mouthparts;
- pull the tick away from your skin gently but firmly—do not jerk or twist;
- save the tick in a small jar of alcohol and record the date and location of the bite on your body;
- wash the bite area and apply antiseptic; and

- see your physician if the mouthparts broke off in the wound or if a rash or any sign of disease develops.

Lyme disease is an illness caused by bacteria transmitted to people by tick bites. Not all ticks carry the disease, but the deer tick found in the Santa Monica Mountains can be a carrier. Left untreated, Lyme disease can lead to arthritis, heart problems, and nervous system disorders. Symptoms of the disease include a red circular rash that spreads outward from the bite, and headache, fatigue, fever, dizziness, weakness, stiffness in joints, or other flu-like symptoms. Other symptoms can occur weeks to years after the infection, including chronic or recurring arthritis and loss of concentration and memory. **If you suspect Lyme disease, call your physician immediately.**

Poisonous snakes

Avoid rattlesnakes. The southern Pacific rattlesnake is a dangerous venomous snake found in the Santa Monica Mountains. (Other venomous snakes here include the San Diego night snake and the lyre snake, but these are not considered significant threats.)

Rattlesnakes are generally easy to avoid and should pose no problem for the alert hiker, but small children must be closely supervised.

Rattlesnakes are important members of the ecosystem and are protected by law in the parks. Your chances of encountering one are slim, but if you do, simply keep a safe distance.

To avoid snakes, always watch where you put your feet and hands; stay on trails; avoid thick brush and grass, as snakes are hard to see there; do not hike at night without adequate light; do not depend on a snake to rattle a warning, as they often will not.

Rattlesnake

Never attempt to handle a poisonous snake.

If a member of your party is bitten, **stay calm and get the victim to a doctor as soon as possible**; don't wait for symptoms to develop. In the meantime, take these precautions:

- Calm and reassure the victim. Few people die from snake bites, and in some cases, the bite does not inject venom.
- Immobilize the limb if possible and try to keep the victim from exercising.
- Do not cut the wound in an attempt to suck out venom. The amount of venom that can be removed by this method is slight, and severe permanent nerve damage may result.
- Do not give any alcohol or drugs.

Wild animals

Avoid feeding, petting, or handling wild animals. Feeding decreases their fear of humans and leads to aggressive behavior. Food intended for humans does not fulfill animals' nutritional requirements and may cause illness or death. Further, even ground squirrels can give severe bites, and carry fleas that can transmit disease. Avoid animals that seem unafraid of humans; they may be rabid or otherwise sick.

Beach Safety

Swimming and surfing

Swim and surf in front of a staffed lifeguard tower. If you visit a beach where no towers are staffed, go to another beach or stay out of the water. Thousands are rescued from near-tragedies every summer month on southland beaches; don't assume you won't need assistance.

Know the limits of your own ability and don't get in "over your head" in water that's deeper, rougher, or colder than you can safely handle.

Talk to lifeguards to learn the safest places to swim and surf; they know the water better than anyone.

Never swim or surf after drinking alcohol, and never dive head-first into the surf.

Backwash

Backwash can pull wading children and even careless adults into the water. Backwash is formed when water piled up on a steep beach face by waves rushes back down the slope to the ocean.

Rip currents

Beware of rip currents. When waves break in rapid succession on the shallow underwater bar that runs just offshore parallel to most beaches, water piles up inside the bar, slightly above sea level. Eventually, this water rushes back to sea across the lowest part of the bar, forming a swift current that can be a major hazard for swimmers, exhausting them and carrying them hundreds of yards out to sea.

Be aware that rip currents can form on almost any beach at any time, though some beaches are more prone than others, and rip currents are more formidable when waves are large.

Learn to recognize rip currents, or better yet, ask a lifeguard to point out areas to avoid that day. If you get caught in a rip current, swim parallel to shore until clear (usually within fifty yards or less). Do not attempt to swim directly to shore while in the current; you will only be wasting your strength, and will likely be carried farther out to sea.

Surf beat

Before entering the water to swim, wade, or surf, spend about five minutes observing the pattern of breakers, or surf beat. Breakers typically arrive on the southern California coast about three minutes apart. Commonly, a series of a dozen or so low waves will break, then three or four high waves arrive, to be followed by another series of low waves. Be prepared to deal with the highest waves.

Sneaker waves

Many people drown each year when huge "sneaker" waves, two to four times the height of the day's average wave, sweep them into the sea. Such waves are formed when two or more wave trains happen to align perfectly in length and duration, and merge, creating one wave with great height. It is not possible to predict the occurrence of such waves by observing the surf, as can be done by watching for surf beat.

To avoid sneaker waves, always watch incoming waves closely when standing beside the water on a beach; supervise children carefully; and stay high above the water on jetties or rock bluffs while fishing.

Stingrays, jellyfish, and sea urchins

Stingrays are occasionally found buried in the sand in or near the surf zone. If you step on one, it can pierce your foot with a venomous spine in its tail, producing

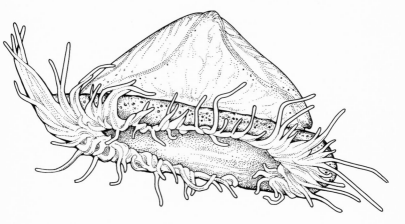

Jellyfish

excruciating pain, bleeding, weakness, vomiting, and more serious symptoms. To minimize your risk of being stung, wear beach shoes and shuffle your feet as you walk in the water, which will warn stingrays of your presence. If you are stuck by a stingray, take these steps:

- Rinse the wound thoroughly with fresh water or seawater.
- Immediately soak the wound in the hottest water that can be tolerated, for up to ninety minutes. This should ease the pain.
- Apply a dry gauze bandage.
- **See a doctor as soon as possible**.

Avoid **jellyfish** and jellyfish fragments; supervise children carefully. You may encounter jellyfish washed up on the beach or floating in the surf zone or deeper waters. Even the nearly unrecognizable jelly-like fragments, typically found on the beach in washed-up seaweed or clinging to fishing lines, can cause burning, redness, stinging pain, or—in extreme cases—blistering, nausea, or vomiting. If stung by a jellyfish, take the following precautions:

- Immediately rinse with **seawater**—not fresh water or solvents. **Do not** apply ice.

For More Information or Special Interests

As an individual or part of a group, you can learn about the rich human and natural history of the national recreation area through the following programs.

- **National Park Service**
  Outdoors, a quarterly calendar of activities, can be obtained by calling (818) 597-9192, extension 201, or by visiting the National Park Service Visitor Center at 30401 Agoura Road, Suite 100, Agoura Hills, CA 93101. The center is open Monday through Friday between 8 A.M. and 5 P.M., and on Saturday and Sunday between 9 A.M. and 5 P.M.

  Interpretive programs are offered to the general public. See the *Outdoors* quarterly calendar for dates and times, or call the Visitor Center. Education programs for school groups are also available. For information, call (818) 597-9192, extension 784 or (805) 498-0305.

- Call the **Mountain Parks Information Service** at their toll-free number (listed below) to receive information and advice on visiting the recreation area, a map of the mountains, and a printout of park and recreation destinations that suit your individual needs—the distance you want to travel, the sports you want to participate in, the kind of environment you are seeking. The service, provided by the Mountains Education Program (MEP), is free, and the phones are generally staffed between 8 A.M. and 5 P.M., Pacific time. Call (800) 533-PARK (800-533-7275); this is a **toll-free**, **English-Spanish** information line.

  Also part of the Mountains Education Program are the Recreational Transit Program (RTP); the Share & Care Naturalist Program; the Urban Naturalists in Training program (UNIT); and the Urban Park Professionals (UPP) program. All are designed to give youth, seniors, and family groups positive experiences in the parks. Advance reservations are required in some circumstances. For information, call (310) 858-3834.

- Soak in vinegar or rubbing alcohol to relieve pain.
- Useful but less effective fluids are dilute ammonia or urine.
- A paste of unseasoned meat tenderizer or baking soda may help in the early stages.
- Apply hydrocortisone lotion.
- See a doctor if more serious symptoms develop.

Sea urchins are likely to be encountered only by scuba divers, or perhaps by beachcombers after large storms. Punctures by the sharp, venomous urchin spines may cause a painful wound, and generalized collapse in extreme cases. To treat urchin wounds:

- Soak the limb in the hottest water that can be tolerated to ease pain, and give aspirin or acetaminophen.
- Carefully remove only visible spines.
- **See a doctor**.

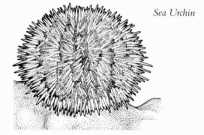

Sea Urchin

- **California Department of Parks and Recreation**: Nature walks, demonstrations, and evening programs at state parks. Call (818) 880-0350, or see the *Outdoors* quarterly calendar.
- **Cold Creek Docents:** Plant and bird walks in Cold Creek Canyon Preserve. Call (310) 456-5625 or (818) 591-9363.
- **Friends of Satwiwa:** Native American Indian cultural and interpretive programs at Rancho Sierra Vista/Satwiwa. Call (805) 499-2837 or (818) 597-9192, extension 201.
- **Malibu Lagoon Museum Docents:** Guided tours of the Adamson House and museum. Call (310) 456-8432.
- **Recreation Outdoor Access for Disabled (ROAD)/ Sierra Club:** This program is staffed by volunteers; organized outings occur at various schedules. Call the Sierra Club at (213) 387-4287 for information on contacting volunteer outing leaders.
- **Santa Monica Bay Audubon Society:** Bird walks at Malibu Lagoon State Beach and other areas. Call (310) 457-2240.
- **TreePeople** (Coldwater Canyon Park): Citizen-forester training and tree plantings; tours of demonstration gardens, nurseries, and recycling center on Sundays at 11:00 A.M. Call (818) 753-4600.
- **Wilderness Institute:** A wide range of fee-based, one- and two-day field programs on outdoor recreation skills, natural history, and cultural history. Some programs for youth and special populations. Call (818) 991-7327.
- **Will Rogers State Historic Park Docents:** Guided tours of the Will Rogers home and grounds. Call (310) 454-8212.
- **William O. Douglas Outdoor Classroom (WODOC)/Sooky Goldman Nature Center:** Outdoor educational programs for pre-school ages, school groups, special populations, and the general public. Call (310) 858-3090, or see the quarterly calendar.

Animal and Plant List

The science of *taxonomy*—the description, classification, and naming of animals and plants—was developed as a way to organize and thus understand the enormous variety of living things. In this system, all animals and plants are classified according to their physical structure. The system's eight levels of classification are arranged in a descending hierarchy: kingdom, phylum, class, order, family, genus, species, sub-species or variety. In most instances, only the genus and species are used when giving the scientific name.

Following, in alphabetical order, are the common and scientific names (genus and species) of the animals and plants included in this guide. The abbreviation *spp.* indicates that there are a number of species in that genus.

Animals
Birds
Avocet, American, *Recurvirostra americana*
Blackbird, red-winged, *Agelaius phoeniceus*
Cormorant, *Phalacrocorax* spp.
Duck:
  Bufflehead, *Bucephala albeola*
  Mallard, *Anas platyrhynochos*
  Northern pintail, *Anas acuta*
  Northern shoveler, *Anas clypeata*
  Surf scoter, *Melanitta perspicillata*
Eagle, golden, *Aquila chrysaetos*
Falcon, prairie, *Falco mexicanus*
Flicker, common, *Colaptes auratus*
Grebe, western, *Aechmophorus occidentalis*
Gull, *Larus* spp.
Hawk:
  Cooper's, *Accipiter cooperii*
  Northern harrier, *Circus cyaneus*
  Red-shouldered, *Buteo lineatus*
  Red-tailed, *Buteo jamaicensis*
  Sharp-shinned, *Accipiter striatus*
Hummingbird, Anna's, *Calypte anna*
Jay, scrub, *Aphelocoma coerulescens*
Kestrel, American, *Falco sparverius*
Killdeer, *Charadrius vociferus*
Kingfisher, belted, *Ceryle alcyon*
Kite, white-tailed, *Elanus leucurus*
Loon, *Gavia* spp.
Owl:
  Barn, *Tyto alba*
  Great horned, *Bubo virginianus*
  Western screech, *Otus kennicottii*
Pelican, brown, *Pelecanus occidentalis*
Plover:
  Black-bellied, *Pluvialis squatarola*
  Western snowy, *Charadrius alexandrinus*
Quail, California, *Callipepla californica*
Rail:
  Clapper, *Rallus longirostris*
  Virginia, *Rallus limicola*

Raven, common, *Corvus corax*
Sanderling, *Calidris alba*
Sandpiper, western, *Calidris mauri*
Sparrow, Belding's savannah, *Passerculus sandwichensis beldingi*
Stilt, black-necked, *Himantopus mexicanus*
Tern, *Sterna* spp.
Thrasher, California, *Toxostoma redivivum*
Vireo, least Bell's, *Vireo bellii*
Vulture, turkey, *Cathartes aura*
Woodpecker:
  Acorn, *Melanerpes formicivorus*
  Downy, *Picoides pubescens*
  Nuttall's, *Picoides nuttallii*
Wrentit, *Chamaea fasciata*

Mammals
Badger, *Taxidea taxus*
Bobcat, *Lynx rufus*
Cottontail, desert, *Sylvilagus audubonii*
Coyote, *Canis latrans*
Deer, mule, *Odocoileus hemionus*
Fox, gray, *Urocyon cinereoargenteus*
Mountain lion, *Felis concolor*
Mouse:
  Meadow, *Microtus californicus*
  Pocket, *Perognathus* spp.
Porpoise:
  Dall's, *Phocoenoides dalli*
  Harbor, *Phocoena phocoena*
Raccoon, *Procyon lotor*
Rat:
  Pacific kangaroo, *Dipodomys agilis*
  Wood, *Neotoma* spp.
Ringtail, *Bassariscus astutus*
Sea lion, California, *Zalophus californicus*
Seal, harbor, *Phoca vitulina*
Skunk, striped, *Mephitis mephitis*
Weasel, long-tailed, *Mustela frenata*
Whale, California gray, *Eschrichtius robustus*

Reptiles and Amphibians
Lizard:
  Coast horned, *Phrynosoma coronatum*
  Side-blotched, *Uta stansburiana*
  Southern alligator, *Gerrhonotus multicarinatus*
  Western fence, *Sceloporus occidentalis*
  Western whiptail, *Cnemidophorus tigris*
Newt, California, *Taricha torosa*
Snake:
  California lyre, *Trimorphodon biscutatus vandenburghi*
  California mountain king, *Lampropeltis zonata*
  Garter, *Thamnophis* spp.
  Night, *Hypsiglena torquata*
  Southern Pacific rattlesnake, *Crotalus viridis helleri*

Treefrog:
  California, *Hyla cadaverina*
  Pacific, *Hyla regilla*
Turtle, western pond, *Clemmys marmorata*

Plants

Alder, white, *Alnus rhombifolia*
Ash, *Fraxinus* spp.
Bay, California, *Umbellularia californica*
Bladder pod, *Isomeris* spp.
Buckwheat:
  California, *Erigonum fasciculatum*
  Conejo, *Eriogonum crocatum*
Bulrush, *Scirpus* spp.
Cattail, *Typha* spp.
Ceanothus, *Ceanothus* spp.
Cedar, Deodar, *Cedrus deodar*
Chamise, *Adenostoma fasciculatum*
Cherry, hollyleaf, *Prunus illicifolia*
Coffeeberry, *Rhamus californica*
Dogwood, *Cornus* spp.
Duckweed, *Lemma* spp.
Eel-grass, seed bearing, *Zostera marina*
Elderberry, *Sambucus* spp.
Fern:
  Chain, *Woodwardia fimbriata*
  Chaparral, *Polypodium californicum*
  Duckweed, *Azolla filiculoides*
Giant coreopsis, *Coreopsis gigantea*
Lemonadeberry, *Rhus integrifolia*
Live-forever, chalk, *Dudleya pulverulenta*
Maple, big-leaf, *Acer macrophyllum*
Morning glory, beach, *Calystegia macrostegea*

Moss, club, *Sellaginella bigelovii*
Mugwort, *Artemisia douglasii*
Needlegrass:
  Foothill, *Stipa lepida*
  Purple, *Stipa pulchra*
Oak:
  Coast live, *Quercus agrifolia*
  Valley, *Quercus lobata*
Pickleweed, *Salicornia* spp.
Poison oak, *Toxicodendron diversiloba*
Pondweed, *Potamogeton* spp.
Poppy, California, *Eschscholzia californica*
Primrose, beach evening, *Camissonia cheiranthifolia*
Red shank, *Adenostoma sparsifolium*
Rye grass, creeping, *Elymus triticoides*
Sage:
  Black, *Salvia mellifera*
  Purple, *Salvia leucophylla*
Sagebrush, California, *Artemisia californica*
Salt grass, *Distichlis spicata*
Saltbush, *Atriplex* spp.
Sand verbena, *Abronia umbellata*
Sedge, *Carex* spp.
Silver beachweed, *Ambrosia chamissonis*
Sugarbush, *Rhus ovata*
Sumac, laurel, *Rhus laurina*
Sunflower, canyon, *Encelia californica*
Sycamore, *Platanus racemosa*
Toyon, *Heteromeles arbutifolia*
Walnut, black, *Juglans californica*
Willow, *Salix* spp.
Yucca, *Yucca whipplei*

Recommended Reading

Natural History

Dale, Nancy. *Flowering Plants of the Santa Monica Mountains Coastal and Chaparral Regions of Southern California.* Santa Barbara, CA: Capra Press, 1986.

Head, W. S. *The California Chaparral: An Elfin Forest.* Happy Camp, CA: Naturegraph Publications, 1972.

McAuley, Milt. *Hiking Trails of the Santa Monica Mountains.* Canoga Park, CA: Canyon Publishing Co., 1987.

McKinney, John. *Walking Los Angeles: Adventures on the Urban Edge.* New York: HarperCollins, 1994.

Raven, Peter H., Henry J. Thompson, and Barry A. Prigge. *Flora of the Santa Monica Mountains.* Los Angeles: University of California, Los Angeles, 1986.

Sharp, Robert. *Geology: Field Guide to Southern California.* Dubuque, Iowa: Kendall/Hunt Geology Field Guide Series, 1976.

Cultural History

Caughey, John, and L. Caughey. *Los Angeles: Biography of a City.* Berkeley: University of California Press, 1976.

Doyle, Thomas W., et al. *The Malibu Story.* Edited by Luanne Pfeifer. Malibu, CA: Malibu Lagoon Museum, 1985.

Gibson, Robert O. *Indians of North America: The Chumash.* New York: Chelsea House Publishers, 1991.

Johnston, Bernice. *California's Gabrieliño Indians.* Los Angeles: Southwest Museum, 1964.

Miller, Bruce W. *Chumash: A Picture of Their World.* Los Osos, CA: Sand River Press, 1988.

_____. *The Gabrieliño.* Los Osos, CA: Sand River Press, 1991.

Rindge, Fredrick Hastings. *Happy Days in Southern California.* Los Angeles, CA: Rindge Family Archives, 1972.

Index